The
Mindful Day

The
Mindful Day

Practical Ways to Find Focus, Calm, and Joy From Morning to Evening

Laurie J. Cameron

Laurie J. Cameron

May you live with more presence, meaning, connection + joy.

NATIONAL GEOGRAPHIC

Washington, D.C.

Published by National Geographic Partners, LLC
1145 17th Street NW Washington, DC 20036

Library of Congress Cataloging-in-Publication Data
Names: Cameron, Laurie, author.
Title: The mindful day : practical ways to find focus, calm, and joy from
   morning to evening / Laurie J. Cameron.
Description: Washington, D.C. : National Geographic, 2018. | Includes
   bibliographical references.
Identifiers: LCCN 2017042264 (print) | LCCN 2017050195 (ebook) | ISBN
   9781426218378 | ISBN 9781426218361 (hardback)
Subjects: LCSH: Self-actualization (Psychology) | Stress management. |
   Meditation. | BISAC: SELF-HELP / Meditations. | SELF-HELP / Stress
   Management. | BODY, MIND & SPIRIT / Inspiration & Personal Growth.
Classification: LCC BF637.S4 (ebook) | LCC BF637.S4 C36 2018 (print) | DDC
   158.1/28--dc23
LC record available at https://lccn.loc.gov_2017042264

Since 1888, the National Geographic Society has funded more than 12,000 research, exploration, and preservation projects around the world. National Geographic Partners distributes a portion of the funds it receives from your purchase to National Geographic Society to support programs including the conservation of animals and their habitats.

Get closer to National Geographic explorers and photographers, and connect with our global community. Join us today at nationalgeographic.com/join

For information about special discounts for bulk purchases, please contact National Geographic Books Special Sales: specialsales@natgeo.com

For rights or permissions inquiries, please contact National Geographic Books Subsidiary Rights: bookrights@natgeo.com

Interior design: Katie Olsen

Printed in the United States of America

18/QGF-QGL/1

For my daughter, Ava Grace

Contents

Introduction

One November morning when I was 16, my father, a NASA rocket scientist, had a heart attack while I was standing next to him. Using strength infused with adrenaline, I transferred his six-foot-five-inch frame from his favorite wooden chair to the den floor and began CPR. Everything moved in slow motion while I breathed and pumped. The paramedics arrived and whisked him out of our home. He didn't survive. He was 44.

I gained a perspective that day that continues to direct my life. Learning at a young age that life can be taken away in a moment left a deep imprint; I perceived the impermanence of all things. Now the rudder that steers me has become one of seeing, connecting, savoring, and fully appreciating every experience. To put it another way, I live more mindfully—and this present, compassionate way of being has become something I practice every day.

After losing my father, I became focused, determined, and driven to live life fully. In my 20s, I became a management consultant with Accenture, and set my screen saver to a banner with the words "carpe diem." I mapped and planned a purposeful course. I moved to what for me was a place of beauty and creativity: San Francisco. I embraced my career as a change management consultant, traveling globally and working to transform companies for the better. My German boyfriend became my husband. We moved to a house near Lake Tahoe, California, and got married on top of a mountain, surrounded by a circle of loved ones. Life was unfolding according to plan.

Then in 1995, my client Chau Yoder saw me as the achievement-oriented consultant in the high-pressure consulting world that I was, and introduced me to mindfulness. In a conference room during lunchtime, she taught me mindful breathing—to stop, breathe, and "be in the present" to simply bring my busy, future-oriented mind into what was happening right here and now. Chau gave me the book *Peace Is Every Step* by Zen master and poet Thich Nhat Hanh, and then she held drop-in meditation sessions every Monday in that same conference room. I started learning how to "be with" whatever comes (a key mindfulness term), without needing to block, avoid, deny, or suppress the hard parts. It was the first time I learned how to direct my own moment-to-moment experience. But I still didn't realize how important mindfulness would turn out to be in my life.

After years of trying to start a family, I finally got pregnant in 2004. It was a time of immense happiness. I had a job I loved as an executive in leadership development, with an office overlooking the San Francisco Bay. My husband and I renovated our flat-roof glass house and took mindful birth classes in Berkeley, learning how to navigate the full experience of pregnancy and delivery with acceptance and joy, no matter what came up. Then in my ninth month of pregnancy, my brother Johnny—a gentle artist—died unexpectedly, just like our father had. He had just finished his sketch for a mural in our baby's nursery. Ava Grace, our only child, was born three weeks later.

Losing Johnny and receiving Ava in the space of weeks was profound. During that time, mindfulness gave me the resilience to be a container for the searing grief and the exquisite joy that I was experiencing at the same time.

Mindfulness is life-changing. It is a superpower that allows you to deliberately direct the beam of your attention instead of being tossed around by racing thoughts and turbulent emotions; to choose your mindset; and to shift how you relate to your experience, so that you have less stress and more joy. I realized that my life had become transformed with mindfulness—from home and family, to how I approached work, my creative pursuits, and what I did for fun. I became determined to infuse mindfulness teaching into my leadership development and change management work from that period onward. This book is a result of that mission.

The wisdom and practices I share here are based on more than two decades of study with mindfulness and contemplative science teachers, including Thich Nhat Hanh, Tara Brach, Jack Kornfield, Pema Chödrön, Christopher Germer, and Kristin Neff. Over the last 10 years, I've been dedicated full-time to offering mindfulness teaching for today's world. As the founder of PurposeBlue, a mindful leadership consultancy, a lead mindfulness teacher with Google's Search Inside Yourself Leadership Institute, a guest professor for mindful leadership at the Robert H. Smith School of Business at the University of Maryland, and a Senior Fellow at the Center for the Advancement of Well-Being at George Mason University, I teach mindfulness to thousands of professionals in the United States, Asia, and Europe and to business leaders, executive MBA students, teachers, university leadership and administrators, physicians and nurses, professional coaches, parents, and more than 1,500 students.

The people I've met along the way—students, clients, teaching partners, and program participants—are part of this book. They became my teachers as much as I was theirs, as they generously shared their own experiences and insights from experimenting with mindfulness. I hope that this collective knowledge of what it means to be truly present will enrich your daily life as it has mine.

This book is your opportunity to see how mindfulness can fit into your life, and to adapt the practice in a way that suits you. As you're starting out, remember that it's not necessary to learn and integrate all of the concepts at the same time. Go at your own pace. It's like learning how to ski in difficult terrain. You start learning the basics; you practice on the easy hills, increasing your skills, becoming stronger, until you find yourself navigating difficult terrain with grace and ease.

Legendary psychologist Erik Erikson observed that "The richest and fullest lives attempt to achieve an inner balance between three realms: work, love, and play." That's why I've designed this book to mirror those realms—starting at home in the morning, and taking you through work, love, play, and back home to end the day, I'll show you how to integrate mindfulness into your routine so that it flows seamlessly into your life and gradually becomes part of your way of being.

We are each living examples of what we care about. And like a pebble that hits a pond, we also leave ripples in our wake by our words, tone, and behaviors. As you give everyday mindfulness a try, think about what you want that impact to be.

Foundations
of Mindfulness

When people ask me what I do for a living and I say that I teach mindfulness, they usually respond with "I'd like to practice mindfulness but I'm so busy I can't find the time." Or "I tried meditating a few times but my mind would not stop racing. You don't know what it's like in here," the person will tell me, pointing to his or her head. Most people think mindfulness is something to add to an already full schedule, a special skill that only a few people can learn, or something that only works for people who have a baseline personality of being calm.

Instead, practicing mindfulness is about learning, bit by bit, how to *train* your attention to stay in the present instead of ruminating over the past or racing into the future. Did you ever tie-dye a T-shirt as a kid? Remember how the more you dipped a white T-shirt into the dye, the more saturated the T-shirt became—richer in color, hue, and depth? So it goes with mindfulness: The more you practice, the more mindful you become, and the more vividly you see the world as you tune in to the moment at hand. In time, you cultivate a different way of being that is more focused, aware, and intentional.

What *Is* Mindfulness?

Mindfulness is the awareness that arises when we *deliberately direct our attention* toward our inner experience, toward others, and toward the environment around us. But more than just focusing your mind, it's about your mindset—how you view the world. Mindfulness reinforces a mindset of being open, receptive, accepting, and compassionate. And that starts with noticing your natural tendency to judge, assume you already know something, or resist what life brings or what is out of your control—things that everyone does.

As you practice mindfulness, you'll start to notice shifts: from being on autopilot, distracted, uneasy, worried about the past or future, to being alert, open, and tuned into the present; from being reactive in difficult moments to being able to take a breath and respond with equanimity and grace; from being lost in thought and judging how things and people should be to seeing things as they are with clear, open friendliness. You put down your ruler and learn acceptance and skillful action.

Your Evolutionary Biology in a Modern World

As hard as it might be to accept, your mind is not present with what you are doing for about half of your life—47 percent of the time on average, according to a 2010 Harvard study. Where *is* your mind when it's not in the present? Often, we are ruminating, worrying, obsessing, judging, or occupied with things that have already happened or might happen: the constructs of our mind, rather than reality. Most of the time you don't stay focused on the book you're reading, the music you're listening to, or the colleague who's speaking to you. We especially don't stay present for strong or unpleasant emotions like anger and sadness. But what would it mean to tip the scale the other way? What if you could be present for even 10 percent more of your life?

By developing mindfulness, you gain back the moments in your life by witnessing and experiencing them with full attention. You develop a way of being that is clear, compassionate, and wise. It's a simple idea, but a profound endeavor in today's environment.

Your brain and nervous system, like the rest of you, is beautifully designed to keep you alive. Because you are built for survival, your brain's own alarm system is scanning for threats and triggering the "flight-fight-freeze" stress response to escape what you interpret as danger. Sometimes the dangers are real—but these days we get triggered throughout the day by a comment, a surprise decision, an angry text, and also by the way we relate to our responsibilities and to the people around us. As a human, your neurobiology is designed to react quickly rather than to thoughtfully respond; to feel stress rather than balance; and to hear your inner critic rather than positive, encouraging words of possibility. Furthermore, for safety, you are built to resist the unfamiliar and to distance yourself from those who don't seem similar to you—in other words, people who aren't in your tribe. This tendency gets in the way of teaming and collaboration, not to mention world peace.

Take these characteristics of our evolutionary biology—we have minds that are wandering, scanning, and getting distracted—and then equip us with smartphones, laptops, and the Internet. The effects are magnified. And to complicate our tech-saturated scene, we are connected more than ever in a world that is volatile, uncertain, complex, and ambiguous (referred to as VUCA), and it is easy to understand the forces that came together to create what *Time* magazine christened the "mindfulness revolution." Mindfulness brings wisdom from the past to provide a remedy for today. That means you can train your mind and body to optimize your experience even in this modern world.

Being Human

Navigating the complex world isn't all that mindfulness addresses, it also helps with the inevitable challenges that life brings—both the joy and the pain. Whether you're falling in love or receiving bad news at work, grieving a loss or feeling overwhelmed by the suffering in the world, you have choices both in *how you relate to* the experience and in *how you respond*. Mindfulness helps you become more conscious of your impulses in those moments. Often when times are hard (and sometimes when joy is intense), our instinctive response is to turn away from the discomfort and turn toward an external escape to take the edge off: perhaps it's TV, pharmaceuticals, shopping, social media, or a bottle of wine. Although you might get relief, it's only temporary. The wiser response is to bring attention to what is hard, and you can do this with mindfulness. Our freedom and happiness are in our power to choose how to show up for the life that is right here and now.

The Science of Mindfulness

Since the first steps in mindfulness research in the early 1990s, the number of studies has increased exponentially. The University of California Greater Good Science Center at Berkeley, Stanford's Center for Compassion and Altruism Research and Education (CCARE), the Center for Healthy Minds at the University of Wisconsin–Madison, UCLA's Mindful Awareness Research Center, and the Max Planck Institute in Leipzig, Germany, are among the cutting-edge centers that are studying the science of mindfulness and compassion. Google's Search Inside Yourself Leadership Institute, which I've been a part of for five years, trains its teachers in the neuroscience that is revealing what contemplative wisdom has long suggested: Being present, focused, and compassionate is not something you are born with or without. These are skills that can be strengthened and expanded. Research has shown that you can change your default mental patterns through repeated practice, a concept called neuroplasticity. In other words, the repetition of mental training in effect rewires your brain with new neural pathways that incline you to respond to situations in more skillful ways than automatically reacting out of habit. You get to be in the driver's seat of shaping your brain through deliberate practice, instead of unwittingly wiring your brain through the influence of cultural norms and your old habits.

People often ask me about the difference between mindfulness and meditation. The two are distinct, yet tightly connected: You can be mindful without meditating, but the research shows that mindfulness meditation is the surefire way to becoming more mindful. Think of it like this: Meditation is to mindfulness as sports is to fitness. Meditation is a body of mental training exercises—and there are many forms—that are designed to develop skills, strengthen your mind, and produce immediate states and long-term outcomes. Research on the benefits of meditation has exploded in recent years, and Richard Davidson and Daniel Goleman suggest that these mindful states start to have lasting effects. For example, the traditional compassion practice of "wishing well" not only creates a greater sense of positive emotion and well-being immediately in the meditator, but also contributes to more kind, generous, and altruistic behaviors. In a recent meta-analysis of the wealth of mindfulness research available, researchers found that mindfulness meditation—maintaining a moment-by-moment receptive awareness of our thoughts, feelings, bodily sensations, and surrounding environment, often using an object of focus—increases attentional control, emotional regulation, and self-awareness. One study found that meditators lose less gray matter over time compared with nonmeditators; another study suggests that meditation may reduce the cognitive decline associated with aging. Meditation has been shown to alter gene expression, lowering the body's inflammatory response to disease and other stressors, and to lengthen telomeres, markers for longevity of life.

In addition to the outpouring of scientific research, stories from meditators around the world attest to the benefits of a consistent mindfulness practice. Mindfulness exercises, which you'll learn in many forms in the pages that follow, can help you stay awake and present and tap into the powers of acceptance, gratitude, and compassion. My students often tell me that they feel more freedom in their daily lives, as well as more energy and a deeper sense of well-being when they practice mindfulness—whether via meditation or by doing everyday activities mindfully. As they gain greater insight into how their minds work, and develop stronger mental skills, they feel more capable of making meaningful choices, and they gain confidence from knowing that they can access a calm, grounded presence on demand.

Here's the bottom line—and the incredible opportunity: You can learn to radically shift how you relate to your daily experiences and to other people. The awareness that arises from mindful attention to your inner thoughts, emotions, and perceptions begins to bring more vivid detail for knowing yourself. This self-awareness is at the heart of self-mastery—of being the person you want to be. It amounts to having a longer, richer life, because you are present for much more of it. And we can all do this.

How to Strengthen Your Mind Every Day

If you've been in a room while a choral ensemble is harmonizing, watched children performing a school play, walked along a stream in the forest, held the hand of someone near death, or looked into the face of a newborn, you know what the energy of pure presence and connection feels like. Everyday mindfulness is about cultivating these vivid moments more consistently into your life—to find joy and wonder in the ordinary instead of waiting for special occasions. Just understanding that mindfulness is a trainable skill is a first step, and now you need to know how to go about it.

Many of us are used to driving ourselves hard, and might think of training as a way to try to force change, to push, pull, and pressure ourselves into becoming something different. Mindfulness encourages a different approach. In this book you will find two main ways of training: with formal, dedicated practices, often in the form of a meditation. You will also find informal ways of training that you integrate into your day. Either way, the central skill is *focused attention* to your body, thoughts, emotions, or surroundings whenever you notice that you're lost in thought. Attention by itself may be focused, but it becomes mindfulness only when coupled with the skill of *meta-awareness*—the ability to know your current state of mind that monitors that attentiveness. And there's another dimension to this: Mindfulness is about paying attention *with kindness and compassion,* instead of judging or self-disparaging. In my teacher training with Tara Brach and Jack Kornfield, they call this loving-awareness.

Qualities of Mindfulness

The following 10 qualities not only guide you toward mindful living; they can become part of who you are and how you see the world. Think of them as attitudes, principles, and even mindsets that support and strengthen mindfulness. Mindfulness is not only about paying attention; it also includes *how* you pay attention. As you become familiar with these attitudes, and practice and strengthen them with the meditations and through the everyday exercises in this book, they will begin to arise naturally as you become more mindful:

- *Awareness* arises when you are alert and awake to whatever is in the moment-to-moment flow of your immediate experience. It's the ability to know, sense, perceive, feel, or to be cognizant of what is happening, which is also called consciousness. Mindful awareness is the recognition of what is present here and now, without judgment. When you are present, you are aware.

- **Beginner's Mind** is seeing things as if for the first time, with openness, receptivity, and curiosity. It's a clear lens through which you suspend what you "know" about an object, person, or concept, and allow yourself to look outward (or inward) with greater clarity. Beginner's Mind is the opposite of being the expert, and makes room for new ideas, novelties, and outcomes. Seeing with fresh eyes can bring back a sense of wonder and awe to people, situations, and moments that have become ordinary—which then invites gratitude and joy.

- **Acceptance** is the capacity and willingness to see things as they really are. We may not always like what we find—but allowing feelings and circumstances to be, rather than trying to resist or trying to force change (which just creates struggle and stress), is a good start. An important caveat here: Acceptance has nothing to do with being passive. It's an active choice in which you learn to say, "This is what life is like right now," or my shorthand phrase "It's like this," without wishing things were different. Acceptance sets the stage for letting go.

- **Insight** is the *aha* moment of clarity. It's the capacity to have a clear, accurate understanding. It comes from experimenting with mindfulness and looking deeply at your thoughts, behaviors, and habits. Mindful awareness helps you see cause and effect in everything you do, and helps you develop a wisdom about how things work.

- **Impermanence** reminds us that nothing stays as it is—in nature, weather, our bodies, emotions, political systems, family dynamics. Yet we often wish things would stay the same. When you see the world as impermanent, you deepen attention to what is here now because you appreciate that it is temporary. And you suffer less when things do change, knowing that you were fully present to connect, savor, and enjoy your life as it *was* and *is* in each moment.

- **Equanimity** is the state of emotional calmness or nonreactivity; it is being aware of whatever is happening without being swept away by it—good or bad. This attitude involves learning to put aside your preferences so that you can be with what's actually there. There is a powerful freedom and a pervasive easygoingness to equanimity. When you cultivate equanimity, life's everyday problems won't rock you and overwhelm you as much, and you won't feel a need to cling to what's pleasurable. It's related to patience, which is the ability to maintain composure in the face of things you don't like, or to stick with difficult situations even when they don't resolve as quickly as you'd like.

- *Interconnection* is a quality of the world we live in, and it can become a quality of ourselves, too. Thich Nhat Hanh encourages us to perceive inter-being with others, with nature, with the entire global ecosystem. This state of mind influences how we care for one another: We recognize that we are dependent on each other, and are cognizant of how we affect our habitat and those around us. We are ourselves, but at the same time we are all each other— people with fears, hopes, and the longing for love.

- *Compassion* is attending to the experience of suffering with the wish to alleviate it. It's applied in the desire to reduce the suffering *of others,* or reduce *our own* suffering (self-compassion). Compassion starts with empathy—understanding and being sensitive to the experience of pain or discomfort—and adds the component of seeking to be of service, to bring some degree of relief. There is generosity in compassion. You can ask yourself, *What would best serve here?*

- *Gratitude* comes from directing attention to what is good, with appreciation for it. There are two components to being grateful. The first is affirming that there are good things in the world, and that you receive gifts and benefits. The second is recognizing that the sources of these good things are outside of you. Other people—or if you're of a spiritual mindset, a higher power—contribute to the positive parts of your life. This reinforces that you're part of something bigger than yourself, and promotes feelings of belonging, interconnection, and joy. Gratitude generates the sense of "I have enough," a springboard for generosity.

- *Joy* is a deep sense of well-being infused with delight. Joy is an innate human capacity, connected to your ability to experience wonder and awe. It comes from within, not from external conditions, people, or rewards. Mindfulness helps you recognize what brings you joy, and what blocks it. And it helps you find ways to access this uplifting quality in everyday life.

Mental Training Basics

We know that whatever you practice grows stronger: For example, each time you catch your mind wandering and then redirect your attention, you strengthen your meta-awareness. Think of it as a "mental rep," just like the exercises you might do at the gym or the drills on the piano. The following are a set of core practices that train the foundational skills and attitudes of mindfulness and compassion. What follows are the basics—and throughout the book, you will discover specific applications and ways to weave these, along with additional practices, into your day.

Mindful Breathing

Following your breath as you inhale and exhale is the basic mindfulness meditation practice that trains attention, cultivates awareness, settles the mind, and calms the body. The breath serves as an anchor for attention that you can use wherever you are. When your mind wanders, you return it to your anchor and strengthen your ability to direct, stabilize, and sustain your focus at will. You will learn about other anchors you can use later in the book—but remember that the breath is always available to you. The following steps are a reliable, natural way to calm yourself and come back to the present:

1. Feel the sensations of breathing: air coming in at the nose, and your chest or abdomen rising and falling.
2. Recognize when your mind wanders, and gently return your attention to the breath.
3. Follow the full cycle of breathing: the inhale, the exhale, and the space in between breaths.
4. Use helpful phrases, such as *In, Out,* or *Here, Calm,* or count breaths to support your attention as you inhale and exhale.

Body Scan

Often taught as the first formal practice for beginners, the body scan is a way to systematically move attention through your body, one part at a time. The best way to strengthen self-awareness is to bring mindfulness to the body, where you start to develop high-resolution awareness of emotions. Most people are disconnected from the body, but as you practice the body scan, you get better at distinguishing emotions by recognizing the physiological sensations that give rise to them. Emotions begin in the body—for example, a clenched stomach might signal fear. Emotions are physical responses to stimuli—whether they are someone's beaming smile, a sudden car horn, or a surprise phone call. As you become more familiar with inhabiting your body, it becomes a rich source of data that can inform and guide decisions. You can do a body scan in a few minutes, or in 30. I recommend starting with about 10 minutes.

1. **Start in a position that is alert and relaxed.** Allow your eyes to close gently if you like. Feel the full support of the floor or the chair beneath your body.

2. **Begin with breathing.** Allow your breath to flow naturally, easily flowing in and out of your body. If you become distracted or your mind wanders during the body scan, you can bring your attention back to your breath, and then pick up where you left off.

3. **First focus on your lower body.** On your next exhale, follow that breath all the way down through your body and bring attention to your feet. Starting with left or right, notice any sensations of tingling, temperature, or pulsing. Turn awareness to your toes, the ball of your foot, the heel, the arch, the top of your foot. Then move up to the ankle, lower leg, upper leg on both sides. As you do so, try to release sensations of tightness or tension.

4. **Continue this process for your whole body up to your head.** As you check in with each part of your body, you might notice strong sensations, such as heat or coolness, pressure, or aching. See if you can observe without judging, evaluating, or prompting your mind to wander off in a story about what gave rise to the sensation.

5. Finally, when you've moved from your toes to the crown of your head, **be aware of your body as a whole.** Take a deep breath that engages your entire body, followed by a relaxing exhale. Bring a gentle smile to your face. Notice any physiological sensations that arise in response to smiling.

Loving-Kindness Meditation

Loving-kindness meditation is a traditional meditation practice that can increase caring and compassion for yourself and other people, according to research. By realizing we all want to be happy and free of suffering, we practice extending good wishes through the repetition of phrases. It opens our hearts and gives us more strength, courage, purpose, and compassion. It also helps us cultivate boundless love, melt the walls between ourselves and others, and ground us in timeless wisdom. By training us to meet our circumstances with an attitude of love and compassion, it also helps us cultivate equanimity. Begin this practice in a natural place, focusing on someone who is easy to love, and go from there:

1. **Start with mindful breathing.** Sit in a posture that is alert and relaxed, with your eyes closed or gazing softly, and direct your attention inward. Begin with a few deep, cleansing breaths, allowing your mind to settle and your body to calm.

2. **Bring to mind a beloved person.** See the face of someone who helps you to feel loved, cherished, and safe. It might be your grandmother, a teacher, or a dear friend. Imagine for a few moments that this person is sending you warm wishes of compassion, ease, and well-being.

3. **Now direct kind wishes.** Do this for the same person or another person who you love and cherish. See the person smiling at you. Allow feelings of well-being, warmth, and love to arise for that person.

     Repeat the following phrases silently:

     May you be happy.
     May you be healthy.
     May you be peaceful.
     May you know that you are loved.

4. **Next, extend wishes to those close to you.** Direct loving-kindness to family members, friends, close co-workers. Using the same phrases, you can gradually widen the circle: to people you know in your company, neighborhood, community, and broader network.

5. **End with yourself.** Repeat the phrases for yourself, which cultivates self-compassion. This is the foundation of self-love and kindness.

Just Like Me

This practice is mental training that helps you to open up and see others as fellow human beings, just like you. Chade-Meng Tan, the Google engineer who founded the Search Inside Yourself Leadership Institute, includes a version of this practice in our programs around the world to strengthen empathy, compassion, and connection, especially in difficult situations. When you perceive others as similar to yourself, you are more likely to have positive feelings and altruistic actions for them. Sit quietly, settle your mind on the breath, and follow the guide below:

1. **Bring someone to mind who you don't know very well,** or who might seem different or distant from you, or even someone with whom you are in a minor conflict.

2. As you hold this person in mind as if he or she were in front of you, **repeat silently to yourself:**

   - *This person has a mind, a body, and a heart, just like me.*
   - *This person has thoughts, feelings, and emotions, just like me.*
   - *This person, at some point in his or her life, has been sad, disappointed, angry, ashamed, or lonely, just like me.*
   - *This person, in his or her life, has had difficult times and experienced emotional pain, just like me.*
   - *This person has experienced moments of peace, joy, and happiness, just like me.*
   - *This person wishes to have fulfilling relationships and know that he or she is loved, just like me.*
   - *This person wishes to be healthy and happy, and have a life of peace and ease, just like me.*

3. **Now take a moment to sense how you're feeling.** As you hold this person in your awareness, what do you experience? And now as you hold this person in mind, send them good wishes: *May they be well. May they be happy. May they have everything they need to navigate this life with abundant resources, support, and love.*

4. **Return attention to your breath**—breathing in, breathing out, and allowing the mind and heart to abide in tranquility.

The STOP Practice

STOP, an acronym for stopping, taking a breath, observing, and proceeding with deliberate action, is a basic mindfulness practice that you can use anytime, anywhere. As the steps indicate, it's about creating mental space to come back to the present moment and shift from reacting to responding. During this process, which is great for times of high stress or emotion, you try to explore what's going on with objective curiosity so that you can determine the best path forward for you. Here's what it looks like:

1. **Stop.** Recognize that strong emotions are present, or that you need to create a moment of space. Just stop.

2. **Take a breath.** Just one breath will shift attention to your body to calm you. This is known as the sacred pause, and you can focus on as many breaths as you need to get centered.

3. **Observe your direct experience in this moment.** Investigate what you're experiencing with your body (do you notice physiological sensations like your heart beating rapidly?), your emotions (can you name what you are feeling?), and your thoughts (what are you believing about whatever is going on? Could biases or filters be generating stories?). This line of questioning is called self-inquiry and helps you tap into personal insights and truth.

4. **Proceed with kindness.** If this is a challenging moment, what would a wise action be? Would calling a friend, taking a walk, or a self-nurturing gesture like placing a hand on your heart help soothe you? If you're with another person, can you access compassion for yourself and him or her by asking, *What would be of service here?*

Take in the Good

When you experience any kind of pleasure or well-being in your life—appreciating a crisp fall day, a refreshing shower, or the first bite of a good meal—notice it and cherish it. Simple pleasures can bring you joy and even a sense of relief. We have many of these fleeting joyful moments in our life, but we usually speed right past them in the daily rush to get to the next thing. Increase the joy by making the wish that other people could also enjoy them. Using mindfulness to rejoice in the good and wish it for others can change how you experience the world, and orient your mind toward the positive. Here's how:

1. **Look for the good.** When you seek out the positive in the small slices of your day, you are able to tap into joy more easily: Maybe it's your child's hug first thing in the morning, a friendly wave from a neighbor, the deep blue of the sky, or an act of compassion that you witnessed. Look at yourself through the same positive lens. What qualities or actions can you catch yourself doing? Being creative, patient, or compassionate?

2. **Take it in.** Fully take in the experience, observation, or feeling, breathing slowly to give yourself time to "install" the positive moment in your mind and body, so it moves from short-term memory to something that sticks. This step is letting it sink in as if you are a sponge absorbing the experience.

3. **Rejoice with gratitude.** Deepen joy by adding appreciation to the moment. Savoring with appreciation is a key to happiness.

4. **Share it.** Spread your joy to others. Draw attention to the moment by saying out loud what is good and uplifting. It will not only incline your experience toward the positive, but will also deepen your connection.

Home:
Start the Day

Whether you consider yourself a morning person or a night owl, you can master how you start your day. The way you wake up can determine whether you feel centered, clear, intentional, and open-hearted—or whether you fly out of the door in a frenzied fog, with sensations of stress already contracting your body, clouding your mind, and closing your heart and perspective. For most people, habitual thoughts rush in as soon as we hit the alarm, and continue to swirl around our heads while we get ready, like a playlist of our own personal top ten hits of worry and planning. We often inhabit morning routines in a sleepy trance, moving on autopilot from bed to breakfast to work or appointments.

But at what cost? Your thoughts keep you from noticing the scent of the flowers on your morning run, the aroma of coffee brewing, or the sweet quality of your children's voices. Autopilot takes you out of the vivid freshness that's available when you're tuned into the present—in this instance, whatever's happening in the early moments of your day.

In the entries that follow, I'll offer ways to transform your morning, which transforms your day. From choosing the sound that wakes you to carving out a few minutes for stillness and meditation, you can create a morning routine that infuses your waking hour with purpose and joy. Beginning your day with mindfulness includes incorporating practices that prompt you to pay attention to the moment, build energy, and savor joy. Journaling, connecting with family at breakfast, and listening to nature are just a few examples.

Throughout this section, think about ways to make the mindful practices work for you so that the habits stick. The temptation to squeeze in a few more minutes of sleep or to race out the door is always there—but taking time to find your center and shift your outlook is worth the effort. In fact, you might find these moments to be some of the most enjoyable of your day. Their impact can boost your mood and productivity for hours after, but most importantly, you deliberately choose practices that support you to show up for your day as your best self. Remember that whatever small steps you take can add up to a clearer, more meaningful, and open-hearted way of living. Life is never the same again.

1

Wake up to joy

Shift from worry and anxiety to gratitude and joy

. . . .

"Waking up this morning, I smile. Twenty-four brand-new hours are before me. I vow to live fully in each moment and to look at all beings with eyes of compassion."

—Thich Nhat Hanh, poet, Zen master, peace activist

For much of my adult life, I woke up with dread. The alarm would sound, and I'd feel a coolness and tightness in my body as worry took over. Concern about deadlines, looming to-do lists, or a neglected relationship streamed into consciousness. I longed to start the day happy and at ease.

Worries in daily life come from ruminating on perceived threats to well-being or concerns that we are causing harm to others. In my case, I was habitually hard on myself, spending my mental energy thinking about what I didn't check off the list, or where I fell short, instead of thinking about what I *had* accomplished, or what I appreciated in my life. I discovered that this habit stemmed from a deep belief: If I am not tough on myself, how will I get everything done?

Your brain has evolved for survival, scanning for threats, ruminating on worrisome thoughts to keep you safe and out of harm's way. The amygdala—small, almond-shaped structures on both sides of the brain—

are associated with sensing and responding to danger. Whether those "dangers" are real or perceived, your nervous system floods with adrenaline and cortisol, which is a natural pattern that can mobilize you to fight, freeze, or flee. It's a natural pattern that helps you escape a house fire, but activated daily by worrisome thoughts can undermine both your emotional and physical well-being, as many of us well know.

Fortunately, there *is* something you can do: Richard Davidson of the Center for Healthy Minds at the University of Wisconsin–Madison suggests that it's possible to train your brain to shift attention toward the prefrontal cortex, where you have greater concentration and self-regulation. By focusing attention with intention, you can activate the regions associated with positive mental states of happiness, belonging, and well-being. With repeated mental exercises, you gradually condition your mind to tap into joy more often than fear. Inclining the mind means to condition yourself so that your mindsets shift from being judgmental, anxious, or uncomfortable to receptive, appreciative, and compassionate.

Being mindful—directing your attention with awareness—is the first step. And mindfulness can begin before your feet even hit the floor, simply by tuning in to the present moment. Start by bringing awareness to each breath, both the inhale and the exhale, as you lie in bed. Allow thoughts to come and go; if you notice worries—about forgetting to buy milk, your kid's audition, an upcoming meeting, or a project deadline—acknowledge them and return attention to your breathing. Resist chasing the thought, planning ahead, and trying to control any uncertainty. Over time, with repetition and practice, it will become easier for you to concentrate and sustain attention. I've noticed in my own practice that my mind is less distractable—and I can concentrate for longer periods.

After a few refreshing breaths, bring your focus to your body, noticing how you feel after the night's rest. You can do this right where you are, lying in bed. Use the body scan practice to guide your area of focus from the bottom of your feet to the top of your head, noting each physical sensation along the way: stiffness, tightness, sore legs from hiking, the spot where you just had dental work—whatever is happening for you.

Practice simply noticing whatever is there, *without* deeming it as "good" or "bad." The intent of the body scan is to awaken to sensations in your body, in the present moment of waking up.

After scanning your body, bring attention to your thoughts—but not the worries, tasks, or to-dos of the day. Focus instead on what you are grateful for. Gandhi said that we are basically products of our thoughts—that what we think, we become. You can imagine a "mental wheel" of gratitude that includes your family and friends, your home, where you live, your work projects, your colleagues, your physical and spiritual health—and finally, gratitude just for being alive right now. Whether you acknowledge help you received, favors, gifts, time, opportunities, kindness, or any form of support from others, this practice of appreciation will help move your mind toward joy.

According to researchers Francesca Gino of the Harvard Business School and Adam Grant of the Wharton School at the University of Pennsylvania, practicing gratitude can have significant results on many dimensions: physical, psychological, and interpersonal. You will notice positive emotions like feeling more happy, and helpful states like being alert and energetic. To amplify the gratitude payoff, you can make a habit of waking up with a gratitude practice once a week—say every Saturday or every Sunday. A study by University of California, Riverside researcher Sonja Lyubomirsky revealed that a weekly gratitude practice is more powerful than a daily one.

What started as deliberate mindful practices have now become my default way of waking up. When I flow through the daily breathing and body scan, and a Sunday gratitude practice, my mornings are uplifting and empowering—and there's a ripple effect throughout the rest of the day. Other small acts help, too: Instead of a startling alarm clock, I now wake with soothing music that reminds me of the deep tones of the Gothic church bells that rang across the street from my former apartment in Germany. In my daughter's room down the hall, upbeat pop music is a welcome signal that morning is here. Choose a tone that brings you joy, and let it be your cue to a mindful beginning. Experiment with a half smile, as Thich Nhat Hanh suggests. Before you get out of bed, bring a half smile to your face, and notice the effect in your mind and body as you start your day.

How: •••

1. **Curate the sound that wakes you.** Program your alarm clock with music or another beautiful sound, such as ocean waves. Give yourself space to breathe by setting your wake-up time 10 minutes earlier than usual.

2. **Take three breaths.** Enjoy three, easy breaths, sensing the full experience of your body breathing, the rise and fall of your chest. You don't need to control each inhale and exhale, just follow your natural rhythm.

3. **Do a mini-body scan.** Bring a gentle, kind attention to your body, noticing any sensations, tingling, tightness. Start at your feet, and check in with each part until you reach the top of the head. Bring a smile to your face, and be aware of how that impacts your body.

4. **Observe and allow your thoughts.** Be a witness to what's happening in your head: Is your mind clear or chaotic with inner chatter? If worries arise, gently let them go—you can even imagine them floating away as if on a river.

5. **Direct your thoughts to gratitude.** Before you get out of bed, direct your attention to what you appreciate in your life. Be specific. You might think in categories, such as home life, family, friends, work, and health. Notice how this practice affects your body, thoughts, and feelings. Each day, be grateful for the simple fact that you are alive, and you have another 24 hours to enjoy.

2

Sit still and breathe for five minutes

Commit to a minimum effective dose of meditation

· ·

"Your solitude will be a support and a home for you, even in the midst of very unfamiliar circumstances, and from it you will find all your paths."
—Rainer Maria Rilke, poet, author

If adding a few minutes of stillness to your morning routine sounds impossible, meditation is even more important for you. This practice provides a calm refuge for the mind and body to recharge, giving you the mental strength and focus you need to step into the day. Think of mindful meditation as a smart investment of your time, offering such returns as being less reactive, less stressed, and more alert, grateful, and content. All of these will help you optimize the rest of your morning and whatever else the day brings.

If you're still apprehensive about squeezing stillness into your schedule, here's more good news: You can practice anywhere, and you don't need special equipment—just yourself. If you commit to just one mental training practice, this should be it. Although you can do this anywhere, I recommend designating a special spot that is peaceful and secluded, if possible. Whether you sit at the edge of your bed, lie *in* bed, settle in a favorite chair, or rest on a floor cushion, having a regular place will help the breathing practice become a habit by removing decisions and choices. And over time, your mind will connect the space to stillness, so that the meditation itself comes more naturally.

As you start out, remember that this is a "practice" in every sense of the word. Human beings aren't used to sitting in stillness, and your mind might start resisting, tempting you with the urge to get up and start checking off your to-do list. You are learning to surf the waves in your mind no matter the conditions, and some days will be smoother—or choppier—than others.

The first step is to choose a focal point for your attention. It can be your breath, an object, or even a mantra—a special phrase you repeat, such as "Breathing in, breathing out" or "In, calm; out, peace." Whatever you decide on, think of this as an anchor to rest your attention amid the random thoughts swirling around your head. If you use your breath, you'll focus on the flow of air in and out of your body, just as you did when you first woke up. When a distraction tugs at your mind, recognize it as just that—interference neither good nor bad—and then return to your breathing. Repeat.

Like most people, you *will* get distracted, and sometimes more thoughts will tug at you harder than others. Distractions are simply nonintentional shifts away from what you want to focus on. Each time you notice a distraction and return to your breath, you are doing a "mental rep"—an exercise repetition for your brain. So what might initially feel frustrating is actually building your capacity for mindfulness; with each return to your object of attention, you are becoming stronger at meditation. You can even say "thank you" when you notice your mind has wandered—because that moment is a moment of mindfulness. This means there's no claiming that you're "bad" at meditation or unable to sit still; it is all part of the practice. And it will be different each time you try it, with new challenges and surprising rewards.

As for those results, meditation can increase attentional control, regulate emotions, reduce symptoms of depression and anxiety, and increase health and well-being, among many other benefits. Meditation quiets the voice in the head and shifts how you experience the moments in your day. It's about detaching from the internal chatter and observing what's happening in your mind and body with a wider, kinder perspective.

Clients often ask me about the minimum amount of daily practice needed to start seeing a payoff. Although everyone is different, remember that just one breath can help ease your racing mind in the midst of stress. But in general, many people see benefits from 10 minutes a day after just a few weeks. What matters is what is important to you. The more you put in, the fitter you become.

If you are just beginning, I encourage you to start sitting still for five to 10 minutes a day for a month. You can increment up slowly after that, eventually having at least two mindful breathing 10-minute sessions a day. You can listen to a guided audio meditation with an app for additional support, or simply breathe in silence on your own, enjoying the exquisite solitude. Either way, set a timer to free yourself from watching the clock.

Next, look for little ways to make this practice feel like your own and help it stick. One of my clients from Marseille, an executive in a global tech firm, sits each morning with her dog in her lap, because when she tried to sit alone, he wouldn't leave her in peace. One day she scooped him up and made him a part of her routine. My teaching partner Hemant meditates on his son's bedroom floor while his child falls asleep. My friend Chau, who first taught me mindful breathing in 1995, lights candles on her mantel at dawn each morning, sits on her meditation cushion, and breathes while holding a string of beads that belonged to her grandmother.

These days I sit on my bedroom floor facing a window so I can see the sky. Nearby are smooth rocks that my daughter hand-painted with the words "Breathe," "Smile," "This is it," and "I love you." Surround yourself with objects that are sacred to you, and that you associate with love, joy, and your own spiritual path. Many people include photos of loved ones, special teachers, or religious icons. Collecting things that nourish you also creates inspiration to practice.

Each day you sit can vary, but it's all time well spent: You're training your mind and body to relax, to be calm, and to focus. Eventually you'll notice that your mind settles more easily on your breath. You might also notice that you have a little more space between thoughts—and that space might be something you carry into the world and use to be more aware of how you feel and act. But what really matters is that each morning—or afternoon or evening—you continue to show up and meet yourself in stillness.

How: ·

1. **Set up a special place for sitting.** Create conditions that can remain constant—the same time, the same place, and the same cushion or chair where you will sit and breathe each morning. Place objects near you that have special significance or meaning. If you travel, create a consistent spot wherever you are.

2. **Use a timer.** Set a timer on your phone or use an app to release the need to think about time. It will be easier for you to "let go" and just sit and breathe if you use an external timer instead of trying to estimate the time yourself. Start with five minutes.

3. **Be alert and relaxed.** Your body posture affects your state. Sit in a way that is both alert, with an upright back, and also relaxed. You want to be comfortable but not fall asleep. Close your eyes or gaze softly at the floor.

4. **Begin with the breath.** Bring your awareness to your breathing, noticing the air flow in and out of your body. Follow the felt sensations of breathing, rather than thinking about breathing. Rather than control the breath, just breathe naturally.

5. **Find your anchor.** Where is it most easy for you to notice your breath? Nose? Abdomen? Make that the focus of your attention, an anchor to rest your attention.

6. **Train your concentration.** Observe your breathing, noticing the inhale and noticing the exhale. If thoughts arise, note them with the word "thinking" or "thought" and gently let them go. Simply bring your attention back to the breath, again and again.

7. **Enjoy the meditation.** Mindfulness meditation is not about striving, getting it right, or accomplishing a certain state. Just relax and enjoy.

3

Strengthen a positive outlook

Hardwire your brain for positivity by practicing
kindness and savoring happiness

· ·

"To make a deep physical path, we walk again and again. To make a deep mental path, we must think over and over the kind of thoughts we wish to dominate our lives."

—Henry David Thoreau, poet, author

What you do with your morning sets the tone for the whole day. Like going to the mental gym, short mental training practices can make a noticeable difference in your mindset, mood, and well-being, which influences what you accomplish—and *how* you do it.

Why take on the practice of training your mind toward the positive? To offset your evolutionary biology. Because your brain is designed for survival, over time, as your ancestors were dodging tigers and other dangers, the default circuitry became more attuned to the negative. We developed neural networks that continually look for, react to, store, and recall bad news. Yet what protected our ancestors can hinder us today. Neuropsychologist Rick Hanson, in a class he led for our group of mindfulness teachers, explained that our brains are like Velcro for negative thoughts and Teflon for positive ones—referred to as the negativity bias. If you find that you cannot let go of a negative comment someone directed your way, or you replay one piece of constructive feedback from your manager among five positive ones, this is why.

On top of that, we not only tune to the negative—we *amplify* it. Our minds spin on perceived threats, losses, mistreatment, and our emotional reactions to them, then spiral into self-deprecating thoughts of flaws, shortcomings, and mistakes, which kicks up feelings of self-doubt. This primes us to be more anxious, untrusting, and irritable with others. If you ruminate about whether something you did in the past was "right," and then start beating yourself up, you are not alone. You are human.

But there is something we can do. Our well-being depends on our ability to counteract this natural tendency to focus on the negative. Cultivating a mind tilted toward the positive takes sustained effort, yet our brains are wonderful, stunningly complex tools, and they can change and adapt—it's that concept called neuroplasticity that I mentioned. You can use your mind to change your brain to change your mind—a principle Rick Hanson drilled into our band of teachers. Whatever you repeatedly say and do changes the structure and the function of your brain. Your neural circuitry can adapt and form new connections into adulthood, upending the previous belief that neural growth is static after childhood.

The American psychologist William James said, "The greatest weapon against stress is our ability to choose one thought over another." If you compensate for the brain's bias by actively looking for and choosing the good, especially the little things that bring you joy, connection, and serenity, you will feel happier, more peaceful, more open and caring toward others, and more motivated for action. When we focus on something, specific neurons fire together, and the more often they do so, the stronger the neural connections become. "Neurons that fire together wire together," Hanson teaches. What you practice grows stronger: Your ability to pay attention to the positive and incline your mind toward greater well-being is within reach.

In the 2015 *World Happiness Report,* scientists Richard Davidson and Brianna Schuyler suggest four components of well-being supported by neuroscience: attention, outlook, resilience, and generosity. Each of these factors, they observe, are rooted in neural circuits that are subject to change—meaning that it's possible to exercise these circuits to strengthen them. This is neuroplasticity at work. It's a pretty profound idea that Davidson shared with us at a National Geographic talk in 2015: Well-being is a skill that we can develop with practice, preferably done in the morning to maximize effect throughout the day.

So take the reins in how you start your day. After your sitting and breathing practice, choose one of the mental training exercises to incline your mind to the positive: It could be any variation of the loving-kindness practice, where you are sending good wishes to others, to an appreciation or gratitude practice like taking in the good, or you can recall recent moments where you witnessed acts of compassion or generosity, which also generates positive feelings and cultivates well-being.

At a retreat I attended early in my mindfulness journey, Zen master and teacher Thich Nhat Hanh observed that we are intentionally "watering the good seeds" of positivity when we engage in this way, rather than watering the negative seeds—both of which are present. He shared the simple but life-changing wisdom that the conditions for happiness are always available to us if we open ourselves to them. It goes again to choosing which neural pathways you want to strengthen. Instead of wondering when a situation will change or wishing an anticipated event would soon arrive, you need only to condition your mind to look, pause, and savor the joy that's already there.

By delighting in micro-moments, you water the good seeds throughout the day—the feeling of tying your shoes before your morning run, the sun shining during an afternoon summer rain, or that surge of excitement and achievement when your team has a breakthrough idea. A friend in Miami snaps a photo every morning of the sunrise from his balcony, which is uniquely beautiful each day. My teaching partner in Sausalito captures the sunset on the West Coast. What are the moments of joy in your own life? The more you start to notice, the more frequently the positive feelings are activated. Due to repeated practice and what we know about neuroplasticity, you will find that you are more inclined to the joyful and positive, changing your brain, your moment-to-moment experiences, and potentially, your life.

How: •

1. **Settle your mind.** First, arrive in the present moment. Be aware of your body, thoughts, and emotions as they are right now, wherever you are sitting, standing, or walking.

2. **Start with breathing.** Practice a few minutes of mindful breathing, which will soon become your go-to first step when pausing, relaxing the body, and directing your mind purposefully.

3. **Gladden the heart.** This variation of the loving-kindness practice is a brief way to counter feelings of being alone and generate the warm feeling of belonging. Bring to mind someone you love. You might picture the face of a child, partner, friend, or even a pet. Smile as you visualize and feel the love flowing back and forth between you and this person.

4. **Loving-kindness for today.** Practice loving-kindness specifically for the day ahead. As you think about what's on your schedule, bring to mind each individual or group of people you will encounter. Then offer good wishes to each person or group by repeating the phrase: *May you be healthy, may you be safe, may you be well, may you be happy.* Do this for five minutes as a minimum effective dose—although you can expand this depending on what is on your agenda.

5. **Take in the good.** Try a "take in the good practice"—and apply it to the roles you hold in your life. Appreciate the contribution you are making in the world. Where are you serving? Bring to mind a central commitment—whether it's raising a child, supporting a business venture, or working on an art project. Ask yourself: What is going well in this role? How am I contributing to it? To install that sense of appreciation and let it take hold, spend at least 15 seconds thinking about your contribution.

6. **See and savor joy.** The practice of deliberately paying attention to the joyful moments in your life slowly starts to transform your day, and your life. Start in the morning, savoring the feel of a kiss on your cheek, noticing the wag of your dog's tail, or marveling at the sunrise from your window. Make it a habit to savor joy throughout the day.

Set intentions

*Consciously steer the moments of your day
and the quality of your heart*

· ·

"Our life is what our thoughts make it."

—Marcus Aurelius, philosopher

An intention exists behind every thought and action. An intention directs you to be in a certain state of consciousness, such as open, appreciative, or nonjudgmental. Intentions are a force—they organize your conscious thoughts and act as magnets pulling your attention toward certain things and away from others. They guide you into optimizing your potential by helping you focus your energy, choose how to spend your time, and consider how you treat others.

Setting intentions is a conscious practice and—like most practices in this book—one you can do at a dedicated time, such as part of your morning routine, and one you can also integrate into your daily activities. Intentions are the source from which your actions spring. They bridge your desire to live from core values (for example, compassion, acceptance, generosity) to shape your daily activities and how you choose to interpret the world. Intentions can be both long-ranging *(I intend to be more generous),* as well as micro-nudges that guide actions *(When I see a homeless person, I will give money).* Intentions help you create a life that is aligned to what matters most to you.

A client in Chicago set an intention to be more present for his loved ones. When I asked what this might look like, he said he wanted to find daily ways to connect with his wife alone, and he would aim to listen to his kids without interrupting. Perhaps you set an intention to be more open. That might mean striking up a conversation with a stranger at the gym wearing a T-shirt with a slogan from another political party instead of staying in your own bubble, or listening with curiosity to a proposed solution from a colleague with whom you usually don't see eye to eye. Intentions start to guide you, action by action, toward a life that is aligned with who you want to be.

Intentions can help you achieve your larger purpose. Purpose is your "why"—your reason for directing the arc of your life and work in a certain direction. Intention is the focus of your attention on making something happen. Both purpose and intentions come from within—they come from your own values, strengths, and what gives you meaning. Mindfulness is about paying attention to the insights that arise when you are present and aware; from these insights you find your larger purpose, and your intentions help you get there.

Although you can set intentions any time during your day, doing so in the morning gives you direction. Unlike goals, intentions are not something you attach to an expectation or evaluation, indeed in comparison to the tangible, measurable objectivity of goals (for example, I will work 20 percent more until I get a promotion, or I will exercise three times a week until I hit my target weight). Goals often put us in a striving, control mindset—whereas intentions encourage us to let go of control, flourish in uncertainty, and allow possibilities to unfold. The specific, rigid goal you try so hard to make happen might not serve you as well as living from an intention that keeps you open to something you might not even predict, like a new opportunity or a door that opens. Western society conditions us to strive for achievement—but intentions encourage us to grow spiritually in ways that make us feel more connected, more aligned, and more fulfilled.

You can also set intentions as part of your mental training in mindfulness. Psychologist and mindfulness researcher Shauna Shapiro finds that our intentions shift along a continuum as we progress in our practice. With meditation practice, we usually start with self-regulation (being able to direct attention and manage emotions) before we move into self-exploration and self-awareness (becoming aware of our preferences, habits, defenses, and conditioning). Finally, we come to self-liberation and compassionate service (being free from the conditioned mind to instead live life from generous love). Consider this continuum of intentions as you take on your own mindfulness practice. After a few weeks of mindful breathing, do you notice a shift in your ability to regulate strong emotions—to maintain more equanimity and less reactivity?

Intentions are more powerful when they come from a calm, centered place rather than from a place of feeling lack, not good enough, or general anxiety, so it is helpful to set intentions in the morning after sitting in stillness and breathing mindfully. When moments of choice arise in the day, stay connected to your center, your inner GPS with intentions as your magnets, and don't give into to the influence or criticism of others or your own self-doubt. Intentions are the earliest forms of your outward behaviors that add up to your life—and as you start to live with more mindfulness and less on autopilot, you become more conscious about setting intentions and living into them.

Intentions come from your wisest self. When you create space in your noisy, busy mind to access awareness, you can tune in to what is important and then set intentions. Ultimately, when setting and using intentions becomes natural and easy for you, you will find your mind taking a pause before any important part of your day to get clear on what matters most. Your intentions guide you—and a clear sense of direction is a source of happiness in itself.

How:

1. **Make it a daily practice.** Choose a time in your morning to set intentions. Make it a habit by doing it just after something you already do, such as after you are sitting in stillness or as part of journaling.

2. **Listen to your inner wisdom.** First settle your mind with a few calming breaths and ask yourself: *What matters most today? What matters most this week? What does my heart long for?* These answers will point to intentions you can set.

3. **Mine your joy list for intentions.** Create a short list of activities that make you feel alive—times when you feel the most aware and vibrant. Some of my joys are being present with my daughter, creating art, swimming in open water, connecting deeply with clients, and teaching mindfulness. You can set an intention to create time for one or more of the activities that gives you a boost, and be open and present when you do it.

4. **Set intentions for seeing, being, and doing.** What do you want to see more? Beauty, wonder, acts of kindness, good news, humorous moments, the glass half full? How do you want to "be" today? Calm, focused, open-minded, patient, generous, accepting, gentle, forgiving? What do you want to do more? Stop and breathe, listen deeply to others, do one thing at a time? Keep it short and simple.

5. **Use ink.** Write down your intentions on a small card or sticky note for your desk or refrigerator to bring your focus back and inspire yourself throughout the day.

6. **Share intentions with loved ones.** At breakfast, talk about what your intentions are for the day. This ritual not only supports the habit of setting intentions, but also lets you connect with your roommates, partner, or kids in a deeper way, and find ways to support them as they live out their own intentions.

5

Reflect in writing

Journal as a process of discovery and self-awareness

• •

"And the point is, to live everything. Live the questions now. Perhaps then, someday far in the future, you will gradually, without even noticing it, live your way into the answer."

—Rainer Maria Rilke, poet and author

It can be illuminating to read what flows from your pen when you journal without censoring your thoughts. Just the act of moving your pen across paper becomes a meditative act, bringing you into the moment that is right here. You direct your attention to the page, open your mind, and make the invisible visible by seeing what comes through on the page.

Whether you write for five minutes or 60 minutes a day, journaling helps you gain perspective and deepen self-awareness—revealing your thoughts, habits, strengths, and ways of interpreting the world. So let your stream of consciousness flow without fear of judgment, and set the stage for insight and wisdom to arise.

Although journaling is an excellent practice for self-awareness, insight, and clarity, it has also proven to be a tremendous tool for navigating times of change, uncertainty, and dealing with difficult emotions. James Pennebaker, a distinguished professor at the University of Texas, has run numerous studies over decades with multiple populations. He found that people who write about emotionally charged episodes for three days a week, 20 minutes at a time, experienced noticeable improvement in their physical and mental well-being. They were happier, less depressed, and less anxious. And the benefits were sustainable—in the months after the writing sessions, they had lower blood pressure, improved immune function, and fewer visits to the doctor. It impacted their performance as well—they reported better relationships, improved memory, and more success at work. When downsized engineers at a company in Dallas journaled about their experience and emotions, the results were astonishing. Compared to their peers in groups who wrote about time management or didn't write anything at all, the group members who journaled were three times more likely to have been reemployed compared with those who had not. Journaling cultivates awareness, understanding, and perspective, which increase your capacity for equanimity when life is full and intense.

Sometimes, though, the challenge is to get the first words onto paper, so try different starting points. Free-form, stream-of-consciousness writing is one way—just taking a fresh page and letting the thoughts flow. You can also try using prompts, or thought starters, to get you going; they give you a jumping-off place for writing. You can use the same prompt each day or draw from a list of prompts depending on your situation or what feels pertinent. Here are some jumping-off points:

What I appreciate most in my life right now is . . .
I am at my best when I am . . .
What brings me alive is . . .
What I really need right now is . . .
What gets in the way of me being present is . . .
If I had no fear, I would . . .
My next best action is . . .

I write "Morning Pages," an idea I picked up from artist and creativity teacher Julia Cameron. In her book *The Artist's Way,* Cameron describes her ritual of journaling first thing in the morning as a way to relieve her mind and create space for new ideas and creativity to emerge. I've been practicing this exercise off and on for 20 years, and I find it to be a source of deep learning about what perplexes me, what delights me, what I fear, and what I long for: questions that increase the resolution and clarity of understanding my own life and journey. These are questions that do not have quick answers; they can help us let go of the need to "figure out" or "solve" things, so that we can instead honor the ongoing process of exploring our existence, as Rilke observes.

To that point, remember that reviewing what you write is as important as the writing itself; it strengthens your conscious awareness. Reading your past entries can reveal recurring patterns and themes, to what is most important for you, to what you care about, and to who you are on the inside. Are you more often reflecting on the joy of being with friends, or are you usually describing the excitement of your role at work? Do you tend to worry about not measuring up? Is there a pattern of seeing the glass half empty or half full in how you interpret experiences? As you journal more regularly, you can use mindfulness to deepen awareness and understanding. Express yourself freely, without standard or expectation, and take in your words with kindness and curiosity.

Students from our corporate programs and in the university mindfulness classes are most often very surprised by the impact of journaling. Many cannot remember when they last took time to put their own thoughts on paper; some described the "real stuff" that came up in a single session of expressive writing. Develop a routine and format that will be convenient and sustainable for you, and get started with five minutes a day—morning, daytime, or night.

You can journal on your laptop or mobile device, but I recommend writing by hand. Perhaps because handwriting is no longer our primary means of written communication, it can be even more enjoyable as an embodied practice of creative expression. The act of moving your pen across paper can be meditative in itself, drawing your attention into the present and synchronizing your body and mind. I also enjoy the beauty of handwriting—it's a unique, artistic form of human expression that can deepen the experience in a way that typing doesn't. But maybe you have your own digital apps for capturing your writing online, or it's simply more comfortable for you. Do whatever gets you going. The greatest discoveries of your life could appear on those paper or on-screen pages.

How: ··

1. **Establish a habit of morning journaling.** Try writing after a few minutes of mindful breathing so that the ritual is attached to another habit. Or keep your journal on your nightstand and put pen to paper for a few minutes before you get out of bed.

2. **Have your tools ready.** You can use a simple drugstore notebook with lined pages, a beautifully designed journal, or an artist's black sketchbook for your writing—just choose materials that add joy for you. I like unlined pages and an excellent fine-point pen.

3. **Create structure.** Set a timer to five minutes to begin. Some experts advise 20-minute sessions. You can increase journaling time over the next weeks and months, but a short practice will help you start. If you don't want to use a timer, you can commit to writing a paragraph, or a page or two. Fences provide freedom.

4. **Set an intention.** Decide what your intention is for writing today. Is it to reflect on what matters most, to clear your mind, or to focus on gratitude to generate a positive state of well-being?

5. **Choose between free-form journaling or a prompt.** Your intention can help you decide whether to write free-form or to use a prompt (and if the latter, to decide which prompts to use). Release any urge to censor or edit yourself; just let your hand keep moving across the page.

6. **Review what you wrote.** At the end of your writing time, read over what you wrote. Bring your open mind, your curiosity to what landed on the page. Do you notice any patterns in the content or in the thoughts, feelings, and moods that it might convey? No critiquing—just ask yourself questions or explore why certain themes might be occurring.

7. **Breathe deeply when you are finished.** Thank yourself for showing up to journal, and check in with your state. Are you excited, sad, energized, lighter? Now that you've opened your mind through writing, this can be a deeply informative moment of personal awareness.

6

Meditate
through exercise

*Train the mind and body with the breath as part
of any exercise that you already do*

· ·

"Nothing ever becomes real till it is experienced."

John Keats, poet

The revelation that mindfulness can happen with movement is often profound for people—especially those who have resisted meditation because they don't like to sit still. If you're committed to morning workout sessions and enjoy the boost that physical movement can bring, you can try turning your activity into a mindfulness meditation.

Runner Ashley Hicks described it to Krista Tippett in a July 2017 *On Being* podcast this way: "I don't run with music, headphones, anything—I call myself a true minimalist runner. Literally, it's just me and my running clothes . . . it's just the idea of allowing myself to settle into the run, settle in and to feel the road beneath your feet, settle in and really acknowledge your surroundings. When I run, it's this idea of really being present and acknowledging where I am and what I'm doing and the purpose."

For devoted and aspiring exercisers, here is some good news. Research suggests that those who intentionally focus on the feeling of moving and deliberately take in their surroundings enjoy exercise more. After tracking how much people exercised, how mindful they were while doing it, and how satisfied they were with their workouts overall, scientists at Utrecht University in the Netherlands suggest "mindfulness may amplify satisfaction, because one is satisfied when positive experiences with physical activity become prominent." What that means for your daily routine is that being mindful can support your exercising habits, and vice versa.

What exactly does mindful exercise involve? You're paying attention to your body: your muscles, pace, breathing, resistance, and tension. How does it feel to get out of your comfort zone and twist and stretch beyond your usual seated or standing positions? How do you feel emotionally? Are you energized and determined, or are you feeling depleted, maybe needing a minute to refresh? Listen to your needs, and push or protect yourself accordingly. Be mindful of your thoughts too. Do you have a drill sergeant in your head? Are you comparing yourself to the person doing yoga next to you, or do you bring a curious, kind attention to how your workout is going?

With mindful exercise, you're also taking time to notice what's around—whether it's the rhythms of the gym or the changing scenery of an outdoor jog. Although music can be a great motivator, and the built-in TV screen on the elliptical machine is nice entertainment, try unplugging for at least part of your workout to truly meditate.

Any activity can work for mindful meditation, and you can find anchors for your attention in the motions: Maybe it's the point when your right hand enters the water while you swim (my go-to), or the contact of your feet on the pavement as you run. Weight lifters might use the up-and-down repetition of a barbell. Or, you could stick with the one anchor that is always available to you: your breath, in and out. Notice as it quickens or slows, and return to it whenever you find your mind drifting to a thought about that text message you forgot to answer, or the milk you accidentally left on the countertop.

Harmonizing your mind and body is powerful. You're making strides—figuratively and literally—for your physical and mental health. And, if the research holds, you're enjoying it more. With that reward potential, a sweaty mindfulness session might be easier to put permanently on the calendar.

How: ·

1. **Set an intention.** Remember why you want to meditate. Is it to train your mind to focus and sustain attention? To learn to navigate emotions? Consider your intention for exercise, too. Is it to live longer, lose weight, or have more energy for your kids? This twofold motivation can help get you up and out, and keep you going.

2. **Unplug.** To meditate during exercise, don't listen to your favorite playlist, talk on the phone, read a magazine, or watch TV. Be fully present where you are: in the woods, on the sidewalk, or on the treadmill.

3. **Attune to your body.** Bring your attention to your physical experience. Are there any parts of your body that are working extra hard? Does your body feel different today than it did yesterday? When I swim, I focus on the water gliding over my body, the muscles in my arms, and the sensation of my torso rotating with each breath.

4. **Notice your breath.** As you learned with mindful breathing, your inhale or exhale can be an anchor of attention while exercising. If your mind wanders, noticing a new "For Sale" sign in the neighborhood while you run or recalling an email you forgot to return, just notice the thought and reconnect with your breath. Observe the tempo of your breath as you work harder and as you cool down.

5. **Choose alternative anchors of attention.** Experiment with attentional focal points other than your breath: each full rotation of your bike pedals, the up and down of a lunge. You can switch anchors as you vary your exercise, but stay focused on the rhythm of your anchor, returning to it when your mind wanders.

6. **Tune in to your surroundings.** There are two aspects of directing attention—focused attention and open awareness—and you can

practice both while exercising. To tap into the latter, check out what's around you. How is the air? Temperature? What are you hearing?

7. **Exercise acceptance.** One of the attitudes of mindfulness is acceptance—not wishing the present moment to be different than it is. Exercising is a brilliant time to practice this. Do you notice any resistance to the workout experience—perhaps wishing you were almost done, or that the pain in your right foot would go away? Commit to your workout time, remember your reasons for being there, and try to stay present from start to finish.

8. **Be kind and generous with yourself.** Notice the quality of your thinking during workouts: Can you appreciate your current ability, speed, and endurance just as they are? If you work out in a group, can you let go of the "comparing mind" and instead thank yourself for showing up for this healthy activity, and then go at the pace that's just right for you?

7

Shower with awareness

*Elevate a routine activity by incorporating
sense awareness, pleasure, and joy*

. . . .

"When awareness embraces the senses it enlivens them."

—Jon Kabat-Zinn, author

How often do you step into the shower in the morning and emerge some time later without remembering much of what took place? Perhaps other people were "in the shower" with you—the people in your meeting yesterday, or the guys you ran with earlier in the morning. In the shower we slip into autopilot, our motions so ingrained that we perform them with hardly a thought—at least none related to the task at hand.

Instead of being present, when you step under the water, your mind races to the day ahead. Suddenly you might be wondering how to get tickets to an upcoming, sold-out show, then pondering whether or not to accept that job offer. Or the voices of family members and co-workers stream into your conscience, resurfacing old conversations or reminding you of unfulfilled obligations. Next thing you know, you're in your towel and onto the next thing. You're clean, but you may feel far from mentally refreshed.

With mindfulness, you can make shower time a personal luxury: A few simple steps can turn this daily activity into more than a routine and engage all of your senses in a way that enlivens you. As usual, it starts with a few deep breaths to settle into your setting—your tub, shower, the gym locker room, wherever you may be. Next activate each of your senses, one by one. See what's around—rising steam, a rippling shower curtain, a colorful collection of bath products—and then close your eyes to sharpen the other sensations. Feel the warm water hit your skin, smell the peppermint soap, and listen to the droplets tapping the tile or the spray of the faucet. Taste might be less interesting here, but consider it anyway: Maybe there's the linger of toothpaste or coffee.

Awareness amplifies the senses. When you live through your senses, you get a rich direct experience instead of a removed experience. You are feeling in the body instead of being lost in your head. Sure, your mind might start to follow a variety of thoughts; the peppermint aroma might send you on a reverie about the peppermint your mom grew in her garden and served in iced tea. When you notice the thought train, just bring your attention back to the immediate feel of the water on your skin, the aromas hitting your nose, and the sounds reaching your ears. Avoid overinterpreting and assigning value to whatever you sense, which pulls you out of the direct experience. Let yourself be in a luxurious moment of aliveness.

A mindful shower might start to become your favorite part of the day, as it is mine. You might discover that you will step out with a clear mind, a greater sense of well-being, and deeper appreciation for this daily ritual. You have elevated the ordinary, and that's a skill you can take far beyond your bathroom.

How: •

1. **Leave autopilot at the door.** Let turning the faucet be a trigger to focus attention. As the water warms up, calm yourself through breathing and prepare for what is an important daily ritual.

2. **Activate your senses with smell.** You can change the order of which sense you focus on first, but for today, use smell. Stock your shower with fragrances that soothe and energize you. Depending on my mood, I enjoy the aroma of lemon and orange or rosemary and mint.

3. **Concentrate on what you see.** Look for details, and you might even find beauty in the ordinary. Is the glass beading with water? Are frothy, shiny bubbles of lather rising on your skin?

4. **Delight in routine contact.** This daily obligation can feel wonderfully lavish when you elevate each act of self-care: Notice the feel of your fingertips massaging conditioner into your scalp. Or choose between a gritty exfoliating shower scrub or a smooth gel, and notice how that feels on your skin.

5. **Think of taste.** This might not be a sense you expect to use in the shower—unless you get some shampoo in your mouth, or you brush your teeth in the shower. But briefly (or longer if you'd like) turn your focus to it: Do you notice moisture, dryness, or any unusual tastes? Don't evaluate, just see what's there.

6. **Soak in the sounds of your shower.** Recordings of falling rain, gushing brooks, and ocean waves are used in soothing CDs and sleep machines for a reason. Water's steady rhythms are innately comforting. If you listen to the streaming shower water for one minute, do you notice changes in your body? Your emotions?

7. **Hold on to that heightened awareness.** As you step out of the shower, think about whether you feel more centered from your mini-mindfulness session. Just as your body feels clean and fresh, let this be like a mental reset for the rest of your morning and day.

8

Listen to nature's symphony

*Allow sounds in nature to bring you
instantly to the present*

● ●

"The earth is a solar-powered jukebox."

—Gordon Hempton, audio ecologist, global explorer,
collector of natural sounds

I live in an old tree-lined neighborhood, and each morning a chorus of birds awakens me. At first I resisted their chirpy greeting by throwing an extra pillow over my head. But then my husband gave their call a helpful reframe: These creatures sing so vibrantly every day that they remind us of how lucky we are to be alive. Even when the wake-up comes earlier than I might like, having that perspective helped me hear their song with wonder rather than weariness.

In fact, wonder is pretty easy to conjure when it comes to nature, and I'll talk more about the benefits of being outdoors in the section on play. But in the mornings, tuning in to natural sounds is an immediate way to ground yourself. This option isn't limited to rural and suburban residents; city dwellers can open their windows or step onto the balcony to hear the hum and buzz below. What matters is that you're listening to the melodies the world around you is making in that moment.

Opening your ears to natural sounds is another way to step out of the spinning thoughts in your mind. In recent years, there's been an emerging trend of activism for silence. But it's not silence in the traditional sense: It's about cutting through our own noise and interference to hear the natural tunes of the Earth. One proponent of this idea is Gordon Hempton, a global explorer who has recorded the soundscapes of prairies, shorelines, mountains, and forests around the world. Hempton views silence not as an absence, but a presence: a means of awakening to what is happening in that moment. He calls quiet places the "think tank of the soul."

Hearing birds tweet, leaves rustle in the breeze, or falling water draws you out of your racing, storytelling mind and connects you with your environment on a deeper level. It is gateway to presence. When you are outdoors, listening to nature not only helps you focus, but also might inspire awe, wonder, and gratitude for this planet we call home—and increase your sense of interconnection.

No matter what you tune in to, the effort is strengthening your ability to direct your mind to present-moment awareness with openness and even delight. This exercise is all about dialing down inner noise to tap into the here and now—by listening to nature.

How: •

1. **Go outside.** This is a mindfulness meditation with sound, best done outside. If you cannot step outside, go to a window or balcony and tune in.

2. **Ground yourself.** Inhale deeply, and send the deep breath all the way down through your feet to connect to the stability of the earth (or floor) supporting you in the yard, on the balcony, or wherever you are. Bring your awareness to the present—everything in your direct experience, the sun on your face, the temperature in the air.

3. **Become aware of sounds.** Notice the sounds around you—the pattering of water dropping after a rain, crickets, birds, maybe the sound of a

squirrel jumping from limb to limb in a tree. What are the qualities of the sounds? Are there melodies? Do they get softer and louder? When your mind wanders, gently bring it back to nature's orchestra. Allow yourself to experience sounds without labeling them and becoming mentally involved.

4. **Listen with your whole body.** Nature sounds help enliven the basic intelligence of nature in our awareness and physiology. Our being resonates with the whistles of birds, the sound of trees rustling, the feeling of a breeze. These experiences wake something up inside of us, and help to reset our bodies to a more natural rhythm. Many nature lovers have discovered this secret without ever learning meditation. See what body sensations you might be experiencing in response to whatever you're hearing.

5. **Invite wonder.** As you pick up on natural sounds, let them remind you of just how miraculous this world is. Let listening to nature be the full experience, without thinking, comparing, or referencing to any other experience, a key to mindfulness. Open your awareness to the entire ecosystem around you: All of it is supporting you and connecting you with the multitude of living things who share it.

6. **Close with a grateful breath.** Breathe and acknowledge how this exercise made you feel. Maybe it brought a surge of joy, or maybe it was just a moment of peace. Thank yourself for making the time no matter what is on your schedule that day.

9
Connect at breakfast

*Make breakfast a ritual for starting the day
being present for each other*

• •

**"When you love someone, the best thing you can offer that person is
your presence.**

How can you love if you are not there?"

—Thich Nhat Hanh, poet, Zen master, peace activist

What are your weekday mornings like? Whether you're getting ready to
head to the office, corralling the kids for school, or tackling a long list of
errands, chances are that preparing for your day is a juggling act. If you
eat breakfast at all, it might be on the go—just one more thing to grab
as you fly out the door. Even though we've all heard that eating breakfast
can be crucial for our health and energy, the "most important meal of
the day" still tends to get short shrift.

But breakfast can be *even more* important than the fuel we get from
food. Pausing to eat or sip coffee with your family or roommates—or a
co-worker when you get to the office—is a terrific way to ground yourself
with your "tribe" and set intentions for the day. You may wonder, again,
How can I squeeze in one more thing before 9 a.m.? The answer is that it
can all happen with a little planning.

My husband and I always appreciate a good latte, and we agree to meet for it at the same time each day. Together we steam milk, grind coffee beans, and make our daughter's kinder cappuccino, a tradition we learned while living in Germany. It takes us 10 minutes—not much time, but enough for us to talk about our day and connect with each other. No matter what you're making—a stack of pancakes, simple smoothie, or bowl of cereal—just being together can turn rushed and frenzied feelings into a mood of loving calmness.

If carving out time for a sit-down breakfast still sounds challenging, I encourage you to experiment with a Beginner's Mind. Let go of assumptions about what mornings are inherently like at your home—and for one week, observe what happens when you set the stage the night before. Then gather at the same time, in the same place, and start the day by really seeing each other.

How: ·····································

1. **Set aside time the night before.** Agree on a designated 10-minute block for the morning meal, so that everyone can adjust wake-up routines accordingly; make this shared meal a habit over time. Mindfulness is about paying attention to our values, our intentions, and the choices we make. Meeting for coffee or breakfast is one of those choices.

2. **Set the stage.** I learned this from my mother. She set the breakfast table for my brother Johnny and me each morning: We had little glasses filled with juice, napkins folded into rectangles, and a stack of coins to buy lunch at school. You can do this the evening before, or have one of your kids or a partner take on this task. Set places with reverence and thoughtfulness, no matter how simple the meal or spread. Your care shows.

3. **Put down the newspaper and the remote.** We love reading the Sunday *New York Times* newspaper on the back deck with coffee. But on the mornings when you're connecting with special people for 10 minutes, put down the things that take your mind away from those in the room. Instead of your online newsfeed, read the face of the person sharing the

table with you. Ask them how they are doing right now. Do they have any intentions for the day?

4. **Take three mindful bites.** Practice mindful eating—even for just one bite, one slow sip of smoothie, or one deep inhale of coffee. Mindful eating is bringing your focus to the food in your bowl and slowing down to eat, using all of your senses.

5. **Be patient with yourself and with others.** Practice empathy when someone cannot make it or sleeps in. New habits and routines take time to get traction.

6. **Notice your tribe.** For a moment, bring your attention to being a part of this group—whether it is family, roommates, colleagues, or regulars at your coffee shop. Our well-being gets a positive hit when we activate our networks of affiliation and belonging, and when we bring attention to the moments of "good" in our day.

10

Create a morning routine

Establish and sustain a mindfulness practice

. . . .

"If I do not practice one day, I notice it. If I do not practice a second day, the orchestra notices it. If I do not practice a third day, the world notices it."

—Ignacy Jan Paderewski, pianist, composer

In 2015, I was in India to teach a mindfulness leadership program at the Google office in Hyderabad, and added a week to my trip to spend time at an Ayurveda meditation and healing center. Each morning at precisely 7:10 a.m., I would hear a knock on the heavy wooden door to my room. I lifted the black iron latch, and a woman with a radiant smile and a tray of teas and aromatic natural cleansers greeted me. For 20 minutes, she would perform a series of wake-up rituals such as rubbing the palms of my hands and feet, pouring a tonic to rinse each opened eye (that took getting used to!), massaging the crown of my head, watching me gargle, and handing me a fresh flower. When she left, I would sit and breathe for 10 minutes, do compassion meditation, and write in my journal. Afterward, I would walk through the garden to breakfast, feeling joyful and vibrant. I wanted to feel this way every morning.

Positive routines are one thing on a retreat, but how do you create a morning routine in the throes of a busy life? It is hard for most of us to stick to doing the things that we know will benefit us, especially in the morning when we are sleepy or feel that a full day awaits. You might often fall into the trap of doing what you feel like doing rather than doing what you know will help you have a better day. Like many of us, you might give in to impulses, like hitting the snooze button or putting a pillow on your head to block the sunlight and try to get back into that dream. By choosing the essential habits that align to what matters most for your mind, body, and spirit, you can create an effective morning routine that becomes your new default way of launching your day. A routine is like scaffolding for your commitments, providing structure and reinforcing the underlying mechanisms that help you stick with what you *want* to do versus what your impulses push and pull you into.

But how to create this sort of structure day after day? Establish habits that support the outcomes you want to create. Habits can be thought of as actions, behaviors, or routines that are triggered automatically in response to contextual cues, like getting in the car (cue) and putting on your seat belt (habit.) According to author Charles Duhigg, every habit you develop follows the same three-step pattern, known as the "habit loop." You can apply this loop to creating habits that bring more mindfulness into your day. The first step is the **cue** or **signal** that tells your brain to do the behavior: For example, *I just brushed my teeth, so now I will sit in stillness and breath mindfully for 10 minutes.* The second step is **performing the behavior,** in this case, the mindful breathing. The third step is the **perceived reward, or benefit,** that you gain from doing the behavior: a calmer mind, a sense of being centered, sharper focus. Here's another example, and then you can try filling in your own:

Cue: Return home from morning run

Behavior: Five-minute body scan meditation and one minute of intention sitting on chair

Reward: Feeling centered, tuning the body, mind, and heart in to what matters most

I think of my morning practice as tuning my mind and body for the day, just like cellist Yo-Yo Ma tunes his cello before each performance. This mindset helps me stay committed; it reinforces that my habits align with my values and are helping me lead a more mindful life.

As you develop your own routine, though, know that although you might start off strong, sticking to new habits over time is the hard part. If you experience this, you are not alone. I hold virtual follow-up sessions with program participants weeks after our in-person mindfulness class, and I hear stories and examples of new behaviors fading out every time. A Washington, D.C., engineer shared that he started off meditating for five minutes a day, and within weeks he could see that the practice was making a positive impact; he felt more present and resilient. Yet when things got especially hectic at work, his practice tapered. He was frustrated; he'd dropped one of his healthiest habits at the time he needed it most. In follow-up sessions, I have students get really clear about the reward part of the habit loop—sharing with others and journaling about the benefits they want to create. Your mind is powerful, and a strong belief in the benefits of mindful practice will help your morning routine.

As you're doing this, focus on the rewards. Make sure your habits are supporting your priorities—your highest values—to keep the habit loop on repeat, no matter where you are or what you have going on. If your behaviors enable a greater sense of purpose, like being more energized to take care of others, the positive rewards of that fulfillment reaffirm the behaviors—and so the cycle goes.

As with all practices and habits, the key is to be agile and adaptable—crafting a routine that supports your lifestyle and personality. If you enjoy travel, know that your routine needs to translate from home to hotel room. If you're a parent, your routine needs to account for the unpredictability of kids. Experiment until you find the set that fits. You are the scientist, running scenarios and observing how your actions impact your morning and the rest of your day. Give yourself some time, as it starts to become part of your natural pattern, and within 10 weeks you should find you are doing your routine automatically without even thinking about it.

How: •

1. **Get clear on the rewards.** What benefits are you seeking to create? This is where you begin in developing a morning routine. Stronger attentional focus? More health? Choose mindful breathing. More insight? Greater self-awareness? Choose breathing and/or journaling. Greater capacity for empathy and compassion? Choose loving-kindness meditation.

2. **Select your cues.** Determine the when and where of your morning routine. What cue will trigger your new behaviors? Hook your morning routine to a specific action that you already do, such as getting out of bed or brushing your teeth, to cue the brain that it is time for mindfulness.

3. **Start small.** Tiny changes breed success in building and sustaining new habits. Five minutes of breathing, one sentence in a journal, a few minutes in nature, one intention—this is how you can ensure that you take the first steps and stick with them.

4. **Say no to tech.** Try not to reach for your technology device until you finish your mind and body routine. Don't fill your head with tasks, thoughts, and emotions, or start sending off requests to others until after your morning power hour. Rather than grabbing your phone, put your hand around a big glass of water to replenish your dehydrated body after a night of sleep. Even better, drink lemon water first thing in the morning. Fresh lemon juice gives you a shot of vitamin C to boost your immune system, balances the pH of your body, and hydrates your lymph system. And you can make it a cue to start your mindful breathing practice.

5. **Post a reminder.** Use a note card listing your routine, and put the card where you can see it easily when you wake. One guy I know has his morning routine on a dry erase board. A mindful morning routine could be:
   - Sit and breathe (5 minutes)
   - Enjoy mindful exercise (10 to 30 minutes)
   - Shower with awareness (5 minutes)
   - Loving-kindness meditation (3 minutes)
   - Step outside and listen to nature (5 minutes)

6. **Track it.** Jerry Seinfeld is known for his "Don't break the chain" method of putting a big "X" on the calendar for each day he spends time writing jokes. Many of my clients find that Seinfeld's method works for setting up accountability: They don't break the chain. I use an app on my phone called Streaks that tracks my mindfulness and well-being commitments. Streaks gives me six tiny Seinfeld-like calendars that show me the streak, or chain of X's, for meditation, yoga, writing, and other habits.

7. **Orient to others.** Strengthen compassion and generosity by dedicating your morning routine to bringing benefit to others. At the end of your last activity, you can simply say to yourself, *May any benefits I obtained this morning also serve others.*

11

Wave goodbye

Be aware of simple moments for generous connection

• •

"Our challenge each day is not to get dressed to face the world but to unglove ourselves so that the doorknob feels cold and the car handle feels wet and the kiss goodbye feels like the lips of another being, soft and unrepeatable."

—Mark Nepo, poet, philosopher

A moment that is permanently etched in my heart is the morning in 2011 that we slowly drove away from our home on the cobblestone street of Oskar-Winter-Strasse in Hannover, Germany. Our neighbors and friends formed a line along the road, waving goodbye until our packed station wagon, with the three of us, our golden retriever, and a stack of suitcases, rounded the bend and disappeared. After seven years, we were emigrating to the United States and leaving the tight band of "family" that we had created since the time we arrived with our infant daughter. The impact of seeing everyone standing and waving until we were out of view is unforgettable. They showed us that we were loved.

In many countries, including Germany, waving goodbye until the person is out of sight is the everyday norm—not just ceremony for a big send-off. It amplifies the significance of what might otherwise be taken for granted as a hurried, routine moment with love, meaning, and belonging. You can easily integrate this cultural tradition into your life by paying closer attention to how you part with the people you see regularly. In the morning, when you or your roommates or family leave the house; when you go your separate way from friends after having dinner; when visiting clients depart the office, pause and acknowledge the time you spent together, and make a final connection with a smile and good wishes. Wait until the person is out of sight before turning your attention to whatever's next. It's a subtle change, but the message that a conscious farewell sends is powerful.

How: ······································

1. **Be intentional.** Bring purpose and attention to the act of separating from family, friends, or acquaintances. Take a breath, reminding yourself of the significance of the moment and connecting to the love in your heart.

2. **Keep watching.** If you're taking off, hold your focus on the people you're leaving behind with hand waves until you're out of sight.

3. **Send them off.** If you're sending off someone else, walk them to the door, see them to the car, and remain standing in place while they depart. Don't start walking away until they are out of sight.

4. **Offer kindness.** Wave with warm eyes and an open heart. To integrate a compassion practice into waving goodbye, you can send thoughts of loving-kindness as they leave, saying silently (or aloud), *May you be well, may you be safe, may you be happy.*

Work:
Seize the Day

It's no secret that top CEOs, NFL teams, performing artists, and Wall Street bankers are practicing mindfulness, as well as training their organizations in the fundamentals. There is good reason: Mindfulness can make you better at work. I don't just mean calmer and more agile, but also more productive, personable, and creative. These are qualities that benefit any professional—whether you go to an office, run an online business from home, work in a restaurant, spin records in a dance club (one of my favorite former jobs!), care for people in a hospital, or any other endeavor in which you use your skills in exchange for rewards.

We all know that working in any capacity has its joys and challenges, from the feeling of accomplishment when you deliver a big project to the emotions that come from dealing with difficult relationships, unexpected challenges, and failures. Whether you're facing a reorganization, a difficult relationship with a colleague, or the cancellation of a beloved project—mindfulness enables you to shift how you relate to challenging experiences with greater equanimity.

The practices that follow are expansive: They will help you develop your attention, regulate strong emotions, cope with difficult situations, generate fresh ideas, and be a stronger team player and leader. They are also simple, starting with how you greet people when you arrive at the office and continuing with how to increase productivity at your desk. But ultimately, these daily strategies help you channel your energy toward what matters most in your job so that your intentions match your impact. As you'll see, these are guidelines for deeper satisfaction with your day-to-day work as well as your long-term career.

The positive effects of a mindful approach to work transcend the individual, too. Mindfulness can improve relationships—one of the most important parts of our jobs, according to the thousands of professionals I've worked with, from the executive to staff level. Mindfulness is the first step in releasing pain points, navigating complexity, and planting the seeds for greater collaboration. As you begin to strengthen your mind, grow your skills, and cultivate positive mindsets, you will lay the foundation for increased engagement, meaning, and flourishing at work.

12

Transform your commute

Devote time during your commute to strengthening mindfulness

∙ ∙

"Nothing is worth more than this day."

—Johann Wolfgang von Goethe, writer

While living in San Francisco and working as an engineer at Google, my Search Inside Yourself teaching partner Hemant spent hours each week riding the company bus on California Highway 101, going from home to work and back again. Finally, it dawned on him that his commute didn't have to be part of the daily grind. He could use that built-in time for mindfulness training and not only maximize efficiency in his routine, but also reap the mental and physical benefits of the practice.

The refrain I hear from people who want to be more mindful is that they have no extra time; their schedule is packed. Sound like you?

If so, I'll share a best practice. Whether you have five minutes or an hour; take the bus, subway, or train; carpool; or travel as a passenger on any other kind of transportation, you can change your commute from a chore to a refreshing oasis of personal time. With practice, you can "take your mind to the gym" while you zip through the tunnels and over the tracks, or walk or bike through the park. And these regular mindfulness sessions will strengthen your attention, bring you fully into the present, and turn your trek to work—or anywhere—into an enriching part of your day.

If you travel with headphones and a smartphone, a guided meditation app like Insight Timer could work well for you. But if you want to free yourself from devices, you can practice mindfulness "unplugged" in a number of ways. Start with practicing mindful open awareness to tune in to your surroundings. It can help to structure your practice with three key domains: sensing, being, and doing.

Then consider your experience through each of these lenses. For sensing, take note of what you see from a broad landscape perspective, and gradually narrow your focus to details, colors, and textures. Then notice what you smell—are there any unusual scents, pleasant or unpleasant? What do you hear? Try to absorb each element with a Beginner's Mind, pretending that this is your first trip along this route. From the people who sit near you to the scenery that whooshes by, what new elements do you notice?

Now turn your attention inward, to your state of being. Are you calm? Nervous? Content? Sad? Grateful? Energized? Consider how your emotions might be coloring your thoughts and behaviors of that morning. Just by acknowledging your emotions, you're already empowering yourself to act with greater wisdom and care—or, even better, to start shifting your attitude if that's what's needed.

And finally, bring focus to the last domain: what you're doing. Are you cognizant of your actions and behaviors, or are you on autopilot, moving trancelike through the train station, waiting in line at the bus stop, or sitting in the car while it's stuck in traffic? Try narrating each step: *I am walking by the shops now. I am sitting on the train. I am looking at the colors of the leaves through the window.* It might sound simple—maybe even odd at first—but these observations take practice. As you build your awareness, strengthening your "observer," you'll start to see everyday scenes more vividly, to detect subtle differences in how you feel, and to be more conscious of how you conduct yourself.

Of course, you can also expand your mindfulness session to include other practices from the book—mindful breathing, loving-kindness meditation, a body scan, taking in the good, or others. See what works best for your mode of transportation and the length of your commute. Whichever approach you choose, your effort to immerse yourself in the present moment can benefit you throughout your day.

Take one of my clients who works in New York City as example. He takes the Long Island Rail Road into Manhattan every day. On the best mornings, he listens to a guided meditation, writes in his journal, and sets his intention for the day during the ride. When he gets into the office, he's in a clear, focused state of mind, and he is more productive and less reactive. But on the days when he instead makes calls or reads emails and the newspaper, he tells me he comes into the office with his mind racing, thoughts unfocused, and an enduring feeling of anxiety. The quality of his work suffers.

And indeed, research by positive psychologist Barbara Fredrickson suggests that your mental states might affect how you perceive certain challenges. When you're depressed or worried, your thoughts about an impending work deadline could be more pessimistic, negative, and hopeless. When you're in a positive state, you might be more open, creative, and hopeful. Which kind of performer would you rather be?

Inevitably there will be days when calls or emails are urgent or unavoidable, and mindfulness meditation must take a temporary backseat. Accept such times with equanimity and return to your practice later that day or on the way home. The present moment will always be there.

How:

When you want to train by listening to a guided meditation during your commute:

1. **Prep your device.** Have your favorite meditation websites bookmarked, and have meditation apps ready to go on your mobile device. See the Resources section (p. 249) for resources.
2. **Get comfortable.** Sit or stand in a way that is alert and relaxed. Put on your headphones and choose a meditation with a run length that fits your travel time.

3. **Listen closely.** Bring your attention to the voice to which you are listening, noticing when your mind wanders or when you get distracted. When that happens, simply bring your focus back to the guided instruction.

When you want to practice mindfulness unplugged during your commute:

1. **Start with your breath.** As with all of the practices, starting with a slow, mindful breath is a way to harness your attention and bring your focus to being right where you are.

2. **Open your awareness.** Move your attention from your breath to your surroundings. Take in the environment of which you are a part. Use your senses. What do you see? Smell? Hear? Breathe for a few minutes and wake yourself up from autopilot as you engage each sense.

3. **Locate yourself.** You can say: *Here I am—on the BART train, under the San Francisco Bay, on my way to the city;* or *here I am in the car winding my way through neighborhood streets;* or *here I am on foot on a busy sidewalk.* Locating yourself is a way to connect to your physical place in the world.

4. **Notice your emotions.** Check in with your inner state. Are you comfortable, or are you agitated because you're running late for an appointment? Breathe and allow emotions to arise without fighting or resisting. You're just noticing—though that simple act combined with breathing might begin to calm your body and mind.

5. **Notice your thoughts and actions.** What are you doing? Try describing your behavior. This is also a good time to notice your habits: Are you judging or comparing your experience (*This car is too crowded; these drivers can't drive!*)? Try to let the complaints, wishes, and annoyances go. You're training to be accepting and easygoing, taking in what's around you without making it good or bad, better or worse than something else.

6. **Cultivate joy.** Your mindfulness practice is more than attention and awareness training; it can nourish you and uplift your mind. Take in the good that is around you, and silently send kind wishes to those you pass on the street or sit next to on the train.

13

Greet colleagues with presence

Create high-quality connections in micro-moments at work

• •

"When we get too caught up in the busyness of the world, we lose connection with one another—and ourselves."

—Jack Kornfield, Buddhist scholar, author, teacher

When I lived in São Paulo, Brazil, in the late 1990s, while working for Accenture, it struck me that arriving at the office there felt different than it did in the United States. It wasn't just the adventurous drive in my tiny Fiat in a packed city of 18 million people; it was that when I walked into the office, there was a palpable change in the time people took to greet each other.

In São Paulo, when you enter any room where people are gathered, including the workplace, you greet each person with a kiss and a warm hello—one at a time, whether or not you know him or her well. For me, it signaled that acknowledging each other was a cultural value. It felt strange because, in my experience in the United States, people rarely looked up from their computers to wave or nod when someone entered the room. I was used to co-workers being heads down and focused.

One of my clients, an attorney in Chicago, explained, "If I were to walk around and greet people, I would be viewed as slacking off or not busy." Many workplace cultures seem to share a similar vibe in which workers worry that socializing is perceived as unproductive. But the secret to a flourishing workplace is just the opposite, according to professor Jane Dutton at the University of Michigan. She says that people need time and space to experience positive moments with each other, and the outcomes are improved learning, resilience, overall happiness, and attachment to the company. In a December 2015 interview published in *Success,* Dutton refers to the moments I witnessed in Brazil as "micro-moments of connection," and she explains that "positive emotions compound quickly, and these short-term meaningful interactions stay in people's minds. It may be as brief as looking at each other with mutual positive regard."

As humans, we are a tribal species, and affiliation and belonging are key factors in what motivates, engages, and rewards us. We thrive when we feel connected to others, and the benefits of that can be personal and professional. In a 2017 report by Gallup, the findings revealed that it pays to promote social connections in the workplace: Companies that actively foster social connections see reduced absenteeism and increased productivity. You don't have to wait for the company to organize a happy hour—you can greet your colleagues on your own.

Socializing, greeting, and connecting with others adds another dimension of meaning to the job, reaffirming that you are part of something bigger than just you and your workload. Neuropsychologist Dan Siegel explained to our Search Inside Yourself teaching team that when we focus on another person, we harness the brain circuitry that enables two people to "feel felt" or recognized by each other on a deeper level. Siegel explained how crucial this is for people, to feel vibrant, alive, and understood. When you tune in to others and the ecosystem around you, that can start with hello. And this emotional strength can help build an environment of trust, improve communication, and promote collaboration.

If, like many places, your office culture is more task-oriented, you can start to shift it, even if starting with your immediate team. Think about what your usual mode normally is: Do you tend to keep to yourself and follow a strict agenda, or do you take time to check in with others before getting down to business? If you find yourself longing for more connection at work, the morning greeting is a great place to start. Say "hi" to each person on the way to your desk, establishing eye contact and actually listening to the responses. Better yet, follow up with people on something personal—a movie or a restaurant you wanted to recommend, or a question about a recital or ball game you remember they were rushing off to earlier in the week.

Try creating positive moments of connections when at work for one week and see what you notice. Stopping to address someone versus hurrying by or remaining heads down is a small moment of choice, but will undeniably lift your happiness and well-being.

How: ·····································

1. **Prioritize relationships.** Set an intention to put people and relationships above tasks and to-do lists. Reflect on this intention during your morning routine, on your commute, and as you interact with others throughout your workday.

2. **Visualize positive interactions.** Take a moment to envision yourself greeting others—saying hello, giving kisses and hugs, if appropriate, and smiling. Then, when the time comes, you are primed to act.

3. **Create micro-moments of connection.** When you arrive at work, begin a working lunch or dinner, or head into a meeting, take a breath and use that pause to remember your intention to warmly greet and connect with others. Turn away from your laptop or phone, make eye contact, and establish a genuine connection.

4. **Reflect.** Notice your state when you sit down to work after spending a few minutes greeting others. How are you feeling now? More connected? More motivated? More prepared to begin work? When you see the reward of connection, you are reinforcing the habit loop that will help you make it a sustainable way of being.

14

Focus your wandering mind

*Increase your ability to harness one of your
greatest resources: your attention*

• •

"A great mind becomes a great fortune."

—Seneca, philosopher

Our minds are designed to wander. Here is a scenario that happens for me: I'm on deadline for a consulting project, sitting at my home desk with my dog, Max, at my feet and the cat, Olivia, curled next to me as I try to write. Suddenly, I realize that I'm lost in thought about yesterday's client meeting. I don't know how long I've been in the reverie, but I can see that the hands on my old metal desk clock have advanced, and progress on my project has not.

Humans are unlike other animals—we are often thinking about anything but the present. We're usually contemplating past events, worrying about what might happen in the future, or imagining things that may never happen at all. And interestingly, this pattern is hardwired. In 2007, Norm Farb and his team found that our brains have two distinct ways of operating: In *default mode*—aka the *narrative circuit* mode that dominates our waking hours—our minds are bouncing from thought to thought and interpreting and generating stories about our behaviors and interactions. The other mode, *direct experience,* is when we are completely tuned in to the present, experiencing the moment in real time. Direct experience activates two key parts of the brain: the insula, the region associated with perceiving bodily sensations, and the anterior cingulate cortex, the part that is associated with switching attention. Although planning and strategizing occur in the narrative circuit mode (planning our role in tomorrow's meeting), the direct experience state (feeling the breeze on our face right now) is what we seek to increase with mindfulness.

Direct experience—being mentally present—is multidimensional. It means taking in your surroundings, your body sensations and emotions, and your thoughts. If you're directly experiencing a meeting, for example, you're noticing the temperature in the room, processing the presenter's words, and detecting the subtle vibration of a colleague's mobile phone or other movements in the room. But this attentive state can be more elusive than some of us think.

In my corporate talks, I like to ask the audience to guess what percentage of their typical day they think their minds are wandering, that is, in default or narrative mode. What's your estimate? I hear answers ranging low to high, but most of the time very high. Harvard researchers found that 47 percent of the time, people are thinking about something other than what they are doing. That's nearly half of our day.

This matters for productivity *and* well-being. In the groundbreaking study that Harvard researchers Matthew Killingsworth and Daniel Gilbert conducted in 2010, 2,250 participants were pinged at random times during the day and asked how happy they were, what they were currently doing, and whether they were thinking about what they were doing or something else. In addition to the discovery that minds were wandering almost half the time, the participants' responses suggested that they tended to feel less happy when their mind was not focused on their current activity. In 2016, cognitive behavioral therapist Hooria Jazaieri and a team at Stanford explored this by taking the research a step further. Their findings suggested that a wandering mind can be associated with less caring behavior. (Note, however, that the silver lining here was that the nature of the mind wandering seemed to matter: Thoughts of unpleasant or neutral topics were associated with less caring behavior toward oneself and toward others, while thoughts of pleasant topics were associated with *more* caring behavior.)

Being present, on the other hand, is correlated with well-being, evidence of which you've now seen repeated in this book. And as we've learned, meditation can be a way to help build your capacity for mindful presence, or receptive attention to your direct experience.

The bottom line is that we can work on taming our roaming minds by strengthening our ability to focus. Now that you understand your two operating modes, take note of which state prevails during different situations in your workday. See how often you catch your mind skipping off to a tropical island while your body is still in your desk chair. Then start using meditation and other mental training exercises (see the following) to help build your capacity to sustain your focus. You might gradually find that frequency of being lost in thought gets lower. But do remember that 100 percent focused attention isn't the goal. Although it is natural and even healthy for your mind to wander—giving your prefrontal cortex a rest and boosting creativity—the key is to be able to arrive and stay in the moment when it matters.

How: •

1. **Use the mantra, *Just this.*** Try to start catching yourself when you get distracted, either from internal or external stimuli. When your goal is to focus and you catch yourself daydreaming, use the handy mantra, *Just this,* to return your focus to the task at hand. *Just this email, Just this conversation, Just this book.*

2. **Recognize and return.** The core skill of increasing your ability to focus is this one—knowing when your mind has drifted off and bringing it back to the object of focus. Your attentional control will get stronger over time. Remember that each time that you notice your mind is lost in thought, you build your awareness.

3. **Label thinking.** Naming your mind-wandering habits is a way to break the trance of whatever reverie you're in, as well as to deepen understanding and reduce distraction in the long term. "Planning mind," "worrying mind," and "daydreaming" are a few examples.

4. **Use your senses.** Reconnecting with your senses is another strategy for reining in a roaming mind. Open up to the sounds in the room, notice the touch of the chair on your arms or back, taste a sip of tea or coffee from your cup. Wherever you are, tap into your physical experience to bring your attention back to the present.

15

Remember your purpose

Purpose provides direction and energy for focused action

* *

"You must live in the present, launch yourself on every wave, find your eternity in each moment. Fools stand on their island of opportunities and look toward another land. There is no other land; there is no other life but this."

—Henry David Thoreau, philosopher, author

I believe purpose is so fundamental to a life of meaning and joy that I named my company PurposeBlue. Purpose is what you aspire to; it gives you a vision of a best possible future and pulls you toward it, infusing your life with meaning and aligning your everyday choices with something bigger than yourself. Blue, in the company name, signifies the clarity, serenity, and peace that are generated with mindfulness. They go hand in hand.

Mindfulness is essential to discovering your purpose. It deepens self-awareness—your ability to notice what activities and pursuits are the most fulfilling to you. It helps you discover the strengths, values, and passions that guide you to understanding your work in the world.

To get clear on your purpose, begin with taking inventory of your strengths and values. Strengths are what you are doing when you are at your best, when you feel the most energy and aliveness. Your values serve as guideposts, the principles and ideals that govern how you act each day, such as honesty, creativity, health, adventure, and learning. Consider what activities and pursuits feel most fulfilling to you, and then explore how those interests intersect with what the world needs. When you combine the two—your strengths and your values—to contribute to something outside yourself, you're living your purpose.

The more your choices and behavior harmonize with your values and strengths, the greater energy and motivation you will have to act in the world. Purpose goes beyond the pursuit of moments of pleasure or fleeting feelings of happiness. In his book *Flourish,* positive psychology pioneer Martin Seligman concludes that the happiest people live a life of engagement and meaning and are driven by something bigger than themselves.

It's easy to lose sight of your compass in the daily hustle. When you're on autopilot at work, fielding requests, attending meetings that appear on your calendar, "getting things done," you might feel frantic, aimless, and even overwhelmed. It is easy to get so bogged down in your daily list of tasks that you forget why you are doing them. That's why having a purpose and finding ways to stay connected to it are so important—the more you hold this in your conscious awareness, the greater meaning you will have in your life.

If you're having a hard time nailing down your purpose, you're not alone. It can be challenging to put into words the deeper things that drive you. Keep an open mind and know that there's no single "right answer" as you consider your unique abilities and aspirations. Your purpose gives you direction and focus, but the path evolves as you do.

If you haven't done so before, try to spend some time reflecting on your purpose until you feel like you could describe it to a friend, co-worker, or boss in a few sentences or less. To get there, start with your list of values and strengths that I described previously. These are the cornerstones of your purpose. Then try envisioning—seeing your life five years from now as if it were a movie. Stretch your imagination and don't be afraid to dream big. After you dream, write it down. Journaling as a tool for envisioning can be a helpful process for self-discovery and insight, which gives you the clues to your purpose. I hear inspiring stories from

Search Inside Yourself program alumni about the impact of how envisioning has helped them discover and live a purposeful life.

Sometimes examples can help. My purpose is to translate the wisdom and science of mindfulness and positive psychology into modern language that helps people live with more ease and joy. My friend Jim, a doctor, describes his purpose as healing oncology patients with compassion. Another friend, Julie, identifies her purpose as creating conditions for children to learn and be inspired, which she does as a fourth grade teacher. No matter your current profession, reflecting on the ways in which your work improves people's lives can provide meaning and remind you that what you do matters. The point is to align your actions with your greater aspirations, no matter the context.

When big decisions come up, your purpose is your internal compass, and mindfulness is the mechanism that helps you check in with your emotions, thoughts, and feelings about those questions. When I get requests to speak at conferences or consult at organizations, I evaluate them against my purpose. If the engagement or event doesn't feel aligned, I decline it. Eileen Fisher, CEO of the clothing retailer of the same name, keeps a "purpose chair" in her office. When she has a tough decision to make, she sits in her chair, which provides a touchstone, or a prompt, to think about the challenge in terms of her company's mission and purpose. Try this—many of my clients have one now too!

Recognizing your calling makes you the conscious architect of your life as you decide what supports your goals and what does not. It brings fulfillment, but it also motivates and propels you ahead. Take stock of how you're currently using your time and commit to those actions, projects, and people that are in sync with your values, strengths, and purpose. Then skip the rest.

How: ···

1. **Start with values.** Think of three people or characters that you really admire. You don't have to agree with all of their behaviors or every part of their lifestyle, but imagine seeing them in action. What is it they are

demonstrating? List the three names, and three to five qualities you admire about each person. As you reflect on the collective list, circle the top five that most resonate with you. Would you add or take away any qualities? Most often what we admire in others is what we value most.

2. **Ask questions.** Get still and listen. *What is most essential to me? What brings me alive? When am I at my best? What do I care most about? . . .* Use this process of self-inquiry and write down whatever comes to mind. (Again, the act of writing can be important to distill and clarify these thoughts and ideas.)

3. **Envision your ideal life.** Close your eyes, settle your mind and body with your breath, and see yourself in the movie, five years from now. If everything is going as best as you can imagine it, what are you doing? Are you serving others? What matters most to you in this scene? Draw out as much detail as you can—sounds, sights, people. When you open your eyes, take a few minutes to write down what came up. Journal what comes up, writing in the present tense . . . *I am going for a morning swim in the ocean before leading a mindfulness retreat . . .* Be bold—this is for you only.

4. **Devise a slogan.** Choose a word, phrase, or sentence that captures your purpose with positive, affirming language. Then say it out loud: *I am a teacher of medicine to help heal; I use my creativity to serve children; I design buildings that protect and nurture.* Once you're happy with your slogan, write it down to make it real.

5. **Embody your purpose.** Purpose is more than a cognitive idea in your head. Get it into your nervous system, your muscle memory, your whole physical being. Stand tall with your feet squared, pull your shoulders back, take a deep breath, and with power, declare your slogan out loud again. What emotion do you feel in your body as you practice this?

6. **Share it with others.** There is power in public declaration (think of a wedding!), and when you say it to others, it becomes even more real. Your witnesses can support you and encourage you along your way.

16
Listen mindfully

Listening with empathy and presence,
without an agenda, is a gift to both people

• •

"To listen is to lean in, softly, with a willingness to be changed by what we hear."

—Mark Nepo, poet, philosopher

"When I'm at work and listening to someone in a conversation or meeting, half of me is listening and the other half is thinking about what I need to do to prepare for my next meeting." A product design executive at a tech company in Paris described his interpersonal habits this way at a mindfulness leadership program I facilitated. His experience is common. I hear it from businesspeople in pharmaceuticals, banking, publishing—in every industry, country, and culture. Mindful listening—focused attention to what another person is saying, without judging or having an agenda—is a foundational skill that is rarely practiced anywhere.

Instead, the ubiquitous listening style today is that the listener steps on the ends of the speaker's sentences with *"Yep, Yes, Uh-huh, Right . . ."* And rather than make the speaker feel heard, this tends to press him or her to talk faster—and around the conversation goes. In our always-on, high-speed world, and particularly in the working world, people seem to get increasingly restless and frustrated while others are talking. This constant, low-grade sense of urgency can impede genuine communication. But with mindfulness, you can be the witness of how you interact with others, and make an effort to add value to the exchange for both sides.

Just as in meditation, the key to mindful listening is to simply notice when your mind begins to wander, and then gently bring your focus back to center—in this case, to the speaker. You train yourself to refrain from interrupting, adding your point of view, or sharing similar experiences. These interjections take away from the speaker's experience by making it about you. Instead of projecting your experience or feelings onto their message, the idea is to listen with the intention only to hear with an open, receptive, nonjudgmental, and compassionate ear. One way to practice this is to repeat back to the speaker what you think you heard him or her say, to see if you fully understand what the person is trying to communicate. You might be surprised by how often your mental and emotional filters lead to misinterpretation, however subtle.

Mindful listening is hard, for everyone. There are external and internal forces to manage, even when you're putting in conscious effort. Noisy, open office spaces with interruptions from co-workers, technology devices pinging nonstop—all these disturbances add to the challenge of concentrating on conversation. And what's happening in your head can be even more disruptive. Start looking deeply at your impulses and habits during interactions with different people. Do you tend to interrupt or "help out" by finishing someone's sentence? If the person you're talking with is struggling, is your immediate reaction to try to say something funny to break the tension? Or maybe there's a silence that makes you uncomfortable, so you find yourself speaking just to fill the void.

We all have our conversational patterns, but seeing these tendencies is a way to learn about yourself from the inside out, and in turn, to know how to be truly present for someone else. With self-awareness, you can begin to listen with greater care—not only to words, but also to the emotion and meaning that the speaker is expressing. You'll not only learn more from the speaker about who he or she is and what's happening in his or her life, but you'll feel more connected.

Businesspeople in my classes often report that they experience an unfamiliar sense of "freedom" when they start to listen mindfully. They notice that rather than being tense, forming their next thought, and waiting for a pause in the other person's words, they're free to truly hear and process what is being said. One guy in a Washington, D.C., class said he felt as if a physical burden had been lifted and he could feel more space to just listen. In the same session a consultant said she could see now how she disengages with listening as she starts processing, solving, and fixing problems her team brings to her. For others, it is as if they let go of being ready to hit the ball back over the net and win the next point. It's a gift to you *and* the one talking; mindful listening is so fundamentally different from how we usually converse that we can feel it in our bodies as much as in our heads. In that space and perspective that you create, you can ultimately respond with greater wisdom and skill—but only when it's your turn.

How:

1. **Set an intention.** When you're in conversation, set your mind to being present, receptive, and ready to listen with compassion. Bring yourself into the moment with a few deep breaths and ask yourself: *What is this person communicating beyond the words they use? What is your sense of what they are feeling?*

2. **Just listen.** When the other person is speaking, just be. Let go of any agenda or points you want to make and try to be there quietly, but mentally active and alert. Use nonverbal signals like nodding or smiling to let the person know you're tuned in.

3. **Notice distraction.** As with mindful breathing, your thoughts will wander. When you realize that your mind has drifted, let go of the thoughts and return your attention to what the person is saying.

4. **Read your body signals.** Tuning in to your own body can give you valuable information about your direct experience when listening. Is there

tightness in your chest, uneasiness in your belly? Or do you feel a lightness and a sense of joy?

5. **Activate curiosity.** When you get fairly good at listening mindfully without speaking, begin to experiment with offering brief verbal comments that express kindness, or ask questions that deepen understanding. The key is to keep the focus on the speaker, not to bend it around to yourself. You might try, "Oh, that sounds rough. What happened next?"

17

Lead mindful meetings

*Use mindfulness to create meetings that
are focused, purposeful, and clear*

• •

"Less is more."

—Ludwig Mies van der Rohe, architect, designer

During meetings, how often do you feel restless, anxious, and even frustrated, because you think you're wasting your limited time? The pull in your body is physical; it's as if you wish one of those cartoon hooks would come in from stage left and pull you out of the scene.

In my years as a management consultant, I've worked in countless companies across industries and have experienced all kinds of meeting formats. Some are focused and effective; others seem to be designed to torture the attendees. Meetings are complex events. The company culture, the personalities in the room, the meeting type—all influence its effectiveness. But the biggest factor in a good meeting is whether the participants are present, attentive, and open-minded.

Whether you're the meeting leader or a participant, you can use mindfulness to optimize that time. According to psychologist Daniel Goleman in his book *Focus,* mindfulness means you are paying attention to what is happening with yourself, others, and the system—that is, the meeting as a whole and the company dynamics surrounding it. It means that leaders and participants sense what's going on in the room in real time, and can respond more effectively. And ultimately, it can add up to more productive and satisfying check-ins that are completed in less time. Try it with your own team.

The key is preparation. Mindful meetings take planning, and the first step is to set an agenda. An effective leader highlights the meeting's purpose and is clear about the intention of each part of the meeting. Take time *before* everyone is gathered to assess what you want to accomplish and what can be done off-line. Think carefully about who needs to be in the room, too. Question your assumptions about the invite list; cultural norms, organizational hierarchies, and office politics often influence who attends which meetings and can override deeper thought about who is really essential. Ask yourself how—or if—each colleague is relevant to the topics being discussed. Is the meeting meant to inform or collect input on a topic, or is the goal to make a final decision on something?

Where the meeting is held can also matter. When possible, try to incorporate movement, which promotes neural integration of the mind and body, and improves performance according to neuropsychologist Daniel Siegel. Can you conduct the meeting while walking outside in fresh air? Apple founder Steve Jobs was well known for his walking meetings, and these have become a favorite for me, too, especially for one-on-ones. If you must be inside, could you try a standing meeting? People are less likely to disengage, use cell phones, and work on other tasks while standing. And meetings are shorter.

Whatever form a meeting takes—indoor or out, standing or sitting, in person or virtual—I recommend starting with a mindful minute—60 seconds of silence to allow attendees to fully arrive at the event. It might sound strange when you're aiming for efficiency, but try it and see if a calmer, more focused conversation follows. If you're the leader, invite participants to turn attention to their breath to let go of any issues or emotions they might be carrying into the room with them. This is like hitting the reset button before diving into a new agenda. As a participant, you can also do this reset exercise on your own, showing up to the room early or taking a minute for yourself in the hallway. Do the best you can with whatever time and space you have from day to day.

Finally, treat the meeting itself as a practice lab for mindfulness, and ask your colleagues to do the same. You can tell them about the mind-wandering research from Harvard that shows that people are generally unfocused for 47 percent of the time and that it's natural to get distracted and pushed and pulled by emotions during the workday. Use the agenda as an anchor, and call out (and ask others to do the same) when there are digressions into unhelpful or unproductive conversations. At the same time, notice when your mind quietly strays and continue bringing it back to the main discussion.

Mindful meetings can also be gateways to bring other practices into the office. As part of the "mindfulness lab," introduce other concepts into meetings such as Beginner's Mind to boost creativity; mindful listening to hone attention and improve relationships and teamwork; equanimity to maintain balance amid controversy; and empathy to put yourself into your peer's shoes if there's tension, imagining what might be at stake for him or her. If it proves to be a fit for your company culture, consider devoting one meeting or a series of meetings to sharing and teaching these concepts, which can then become part of your team's standard practices.

I've seen the shifts that can occur for individuals and teams in more mindful meetings countless times now, but one example stands out: A client in commercial sales for an IT company in New York confided that he dreaded the mandatory management meetings held every Monday morning. Sometimes he would be connected and energized, but often he would feel restless, distracted, and generally negative about the company. On those days, he found himself harshly judging his colleagues' comments.

So, for six weeks I suggested he work with the idea of an imaginary line to stay in tune with his physical and emotional state during these meetings, a metaphor from Joseph Campbell and now widely used in teaching how to be a more mindful leader. He imagined his conscious state divided by a line. When he felt alert, curious, and optimistic, he was "above the line"; when he felt bored, judgmental, or cynical, he was "below the line." Each time he found himself below the line, my client was to bring attention to his breath, the sounds in the room, and his intention for being there. He taught this mental mindfulness tool to his team and the broader management group, and now they have a common language to talk about their level of presence and engagement. *I just got off the phone with the client—and I am so below the line!*

By having a neutral way of thinking about our natural states, we can become more conscious, and help others in our meetings do the same. At the end of the experiment, my client reported that he no longer felt "subject" to that dreaded morning meeting. Instead, he felt energized, and he noticed that his enthusiasm was contagious. By sharing and naming the mental practice, he normalized what many of us experience—and elevated the group as a whole.

How:

1. **Begin with breathing.** Most people rush from meeting to meeting, so making time for people to settle in will help attendees become present and focused. CEO Eileen Fisher keeps brass hand chimes in each conference room. At the start of each meeting, someone sounds the chime and everyone takes a minute or two to breathe. At Deloitte, we introduced mindful meeting guidelines, so anyone can do the same ritual using a phone timer.

2. **Conduct a quick check-in.** Instead of diving right into the agenda, check in with each person in the room by asking: *On a scale of 1 to 5, how present are you right now?* If participants wish to share, they can briefly mention what is going on that is in the way of their answering with a "5"—such as a parent in surgery or a "work fire" that is still smoldering. Or simply ask "What has your attention?" This check-in works well for virtual meetings, too. If you're the meeting leader, you start and set a time limit of 1-2 minutes.

3. **Clarify purpose.** Before reading the agenda, state the reason you called the meeting: the intention for each topic, or the outcomes you are

seeking. Perhaps you wanted to get everyone on the same page, to gather input, or to strengthen team connections. Specify what the approach will be to each agenda item, whether brainstorming, voting on big decisions, or open discussion. Always close with next steps. If you're the attendee, ask questions to clarify purpose, roles, and desired results.

4. **Review your own mindful meeting practices.** Be present, and listen with openness, receptivity, and an attitude of compassion for others. When you notice your mind wandering, return attention to the conversation. If you feel yourself becoming judgmental or negatively triggered by what someone else is saying, focus on your breath to calm your mind and body. Then consider what grabbed you and why. Could it be part of a story in your head, or touching an old wound?

5. **Close with appreciation.** When you give meeting participants credit for what was accomplished—agreements made, deeper understanding, actions assigned—they will leave in a positive and inspired state of mind.

18

Email and text mindfully

Use email and texts to increase productivity, focus, and compassionate communication

● ●

"Look before you leap."

—Early English proverb

Have you ever fired off an email or text message at work and felt sudden weight in your stomach after pressing send? You wish you could turn on a magical digital vacuum and pull it back. We've all been there.

Emailing and texting are becoming more common than voice-to-voice communication. In fact, digital interactions most likely consume a good portion of your workday. A McKinsey Global Institute study in 2012 found that employees spend 28 percent of their workweek just checking emails. That might not surprise you. Part of our challenge at work is navigating the sheer volume of incoming information, and each new bolded email in your inbox or text alert on your phone triggers a twitch of curiosity. Your buzzing and beeping devices, although helpful for communication, can also be a continual temptation and distraction.

There's another challenge with emails and texts. With the exchange of only words, you miss out on a significant part of human interaction. Think about having a face-to-face conversation: Much of the intent, meaning, and mood you want to convey comes through the quality of your voice, the twinkle in your eyes, or your facial expressions. In digital conversations, those cues are missing. Reading a text from your boss that says, "Meet me in my office at 3" can kick the alarm system in your brain—the amygdala—into gear, activating your stress response in seconds because the invite sounds somehow ominous. Psychologist Daniel Goleman calls this "the amygdala hijack." If you could have heard the tone of your boss's voice or have seen his or her smiling face, you might have been tipped off that the meeting was actually about nominating you for an award.

Common themes trigger us at work, according to David Rock, head of the Neuroleadership Institute. We can feel that clench in the stomach or that flush in the face almost immediately, particularly when we perceive threats to our status, certainty, autonomy, relatedness, or fairness—referred to as the SCARF model. If you are seeking validation and approval—as most people are—and instead get the opposite, that's also a potential trigger. Mindfulness can help—not only with your self-awareness in what triggers you and in how you engage, but in how you manage your workflow, energy, and emails in general, so that you aren't reading "loaded" messages in higher stress moments when you're more susceptible to provocation. Try designating time for checking email at intervals throughout the day, and disconnecting for the rest of the time if you can, approaching emails when you are in a more grounded, centered state. This is likely to make you more efficient at other tasks in addition to giving you greater clarity and purpose when you do check your inbox.

If a worrisome email or text does pop up then, give yourself the time, space, and focus to consider *why* it bothered you. Start with one minute of mindful breathing, then look at what you're assuming about the message content and the intention of the sender—are any of those patterns from SCARF, such as autonomy, or fairness, in play? Or is there a misalignment of values, priorities, or a misunderstanding? Depending on how "charged" the message makes you feel, you might wait minutes, hours, or even days before you respond. But as you know now, this process of pausing and reflecting allows your rational, thinking mind to step back in.

As you consider the perspective and intentions of the sender, remember that there is a person just like you behind whatever appears on your device. A key tenet of mindfulness is to be aware of what's going on with others, and this can be made more challenging when we aren't standing in the room together, but are reading nonverbal cues and sensing the mood. When you can focus on how others are just like you, instead of seeing them as "other," you increase your empathy and prosocial ability. And empathy is essential when crafting responses to what might be upsetting emails or texts—it creates an opening for collaboration and resolution. As you review messages, ask yourself the following of whomever you are communicating with:

- *What are his or her concerns and needs?*
- *What is at stake for him or her?*
- *What outcome is he or she after?*

With deeper understanding and wider perspective, you can demonstrate to your colleague or client that you heard his or her request and then clearly state your own intentions without words of defensiveness or blame. Try going a step further and crafting the email in a way that would give the other person some relief, which brings in compassion. A compassionate email seeks to ease the burden of others—it's not meant to win, be right, or prove a point.

Working together requires navigating intense emotions at times. We are human, and—especially when the stakes are high, people are stressed, energy is low—there is fertile ground for misunderstandings, unclear communication, hurt feelings, and unintended consequences. When that suffering is met with empathy and care, then compassion is present, which benefits the individuals and the organization. Jane Dutton and her team at University of Michigan's CompassionLab compiled a review of the body of research on compassion at work, and found that when people experience more compassion at work, they feel more valued and worthy, have higher levels of shared positive emotion, greater collective commitment, lower turnover rates, and greater collaboration. Compassion builds trust, and when emails and texts are written with attention to others, perspective taking, and the wish to demonstrate care and relieve suffering, the outcomes are stronger relationships, connection, and trust. As work becomes more virtual, platform-, email-, and text-based, becoming better at compassionate communication is more essential than ever.

How: •••••••••••••••••••••••••••••••••••••••

1. **Notice your impulses and habits.** Pay attention to the urge to check email or text. The next time you feel compelled to check for new messages, notice what the impulse feels like in your body, and allow it to pass, staying present with whatever you were doing. You can break what is becoming for many an addiction to checking messages.

2. **Plan email time.** Experiment with establishing certain times a day when you check, respond to, and write messages. For example, having three designated email times might give you peace of mind if you feel anxious about only checking periodically, while also setting expectations with others that you are not "always on" 24/7, if that's possible in your role.

3. **Reflect before you write.** When you start to draft an email, pause and take a breath. What is your mental state and mood? Is this the best time to write this message? Is this a communication that is too nuanced, complicated, or issue-laden for written communication, and that would be better handled in a face-to-face or phone conversation? If so, walk over to the person's work space, pick up the phone, or schedule a call.

4. **Check intentions.** When you begin an email, consider your intention. What outcome are you hoping for? Connection? Delegation? Confirmation? Agreement? Help? Make your message tone and content match your intention.

5. **Take the other person's perspective.** Imagine how the receiver of your message might interpret it. Try to understand what's at stake for the

other person and how they might feel. Make the intention of your message match the impact on the receiver by thoughtfully choosing words instead of rushing. What would a compassionate email or text from you look like in this situation?

6. **Draft and wait.** When crafting a response to something difficult you received, or when addressing something that is sensitive (and a phone call is not possible), draft the email and hit save before sending it. Return to it the next day—or even an hour later—and read it as if you were the recipient. You might decide not to send it at all.

19

Keep an open mind

A curious, receptive mind is the birthplace of ideas,
innovation, and collaboration

· ·

"In the beginner's mind there are many possibilities. In the expert's mind there are few."

—Shunryu Suzuki, Japanese Zen priest, author

What does having an open mind mean to you? Most of us like to consider ourselves as open-minded—as being flexible in our thinking and adaptive in our opinions and points of view.

But what you see and how you see it might have more room for growth than you realize. Take labeling, for example. As a child, adults likely taught you by pointing to objects and naming them for you: *Tree! Plane! Dog!* You were learning to communicate, but as you filed the words in your memory, they came with sensory and emotional attachments. Imagine how the same thing might happen at work. What associations come to mind when you hear terms and labels like *new hire, deadline, status report, code, boss?* Do certain assumptions arise?

We all have subconscious filters that influence our perception—underlying attitudes and stereotypes that affect our judgment and behavior—even if we aren't aware it's happening. Scientists using MRI technology have identified what's known as implicit bias as an automatic neurological response that's measurable in the brain. This makes sense from an evolutionary standpoint: Our brains are designed to make mental maps, models, and labels for efficiency. The processing framework allows us to evaluate our surroundings and conduct ourselves using less brainpower, thereby conserving precious energy. Yet this mental proficiency can be a hindrance, too. Our preconceived notions and shortcuts can block us from other ideas and possibilities. If we never move beyond these constructs, never reexamine "what is" or take different perspectives, our worldview is confined.

On top of that, our moods can be restricting too. According to research, when you are anxious, frustrated, angry, or fearful, your range of awareness narrows. Negativity restricts your brain to a narrow view, while positive emotions widen your span of attention. As psychologist Barbara Fredrickson, an expert in positive psychology, describes it, when you are feeling good, your awareness expands from your usual self-centered focus on "me" to a more inclusive and broader focus on "we." A "we mindset" embraces a broader set of possibilities.

Cultivating an open mind at work requires you to question your own opinions and patterns. Sounds tricky, but you can train your brain to do this better and more often. The first step is observing your tendency to judge (yes, we all do it). For one day, see what value you might be assigning to the people, objects, and ideas you encounter: from how your co-worker reacts to a difficult phone call to how your boss delivers a presentation. Look inward, too. Are there voices of self-judging, cynicism, or fear that underpin your ability to stretch to new ideas, possibilities, and innovations?

Otto Scharmer, the founder of the Presencing Institute and an MIT professor, suggests that identifying and letting go of our restricting inner voices can help us become more open and present, and thus more creative and collaborative. Scharmer uses the term "presencing"—combining "present" with "sensing"—to describe the process of coming into the moment and activating full, uninhibited awareness.

Scharmer's approach is a powerful example of applied mindfulness at work. When facilitating groups, stakeholders in a conflict, and even governments, Scharmer uses a U-curve model as a way to systemically guide participants from a closed mind to an open one. When you are actively "presencing," your interior state is open-minded and receptive to new ideas, aware and sensing what is happening in the moment without bias and judgment. Mindfulness helps with recognizing and suspending the voices in your head that keep you attached and stuck, reduce your motivation, and shut down your willingness to stretch and see differently. Scharmer and his colleagues call these the Voice of Judgment *(That is a bad idea)*, the Voice of Cynicism *(That will never work here)*, and the Voice of Fear *(There will be negative consequences)*. Letting go of these limiting voices, you hit the bottom of the U—and in that sweet spot, you are more able to see with fresh eyes. We let ideas flow freely, and then practice crystalizing these visions into concepts and intentions that we can enact and share. Doing so is the other end of the U, and it means that we have shifted from limiting, ego-based thinking to a more receptive, outwardly connected state that reflects an open will, open heart, and open mind.

Not only do our inner voices block our open mind, but we also have the obstacle of our biases. A 2015 article in *Smithsonian* magazine suggests that biases can be unlearned, but it is not easy. The first step is awareness—you have to be able to see your biases and then do something about them.

Mindfulness meditation helps here. In a 2015 Harvard study researchers found that mindfulness meditation may help reduce bias. They suggest that by concentrating on the present, you are less likely to be compelled by automatic evaluations based on old associations, and more likely to respond thoughtfully.

Professor Debashis Chatterjee, an expert in the field of conscious leadership in India, reminds us that great masters in ancient civilizations were known as seers. They saw the world around them with what was revered as preternatural perspective. The same might be said of many inventors and thought leaders—but you might say their real power was an open mind. An open mind is what enabled Galileo Galilei to consider that the sun might actually be the center of the solar system, and Sir Isaac Newton to see more than just a falling apple, as everyone else saw before him, when he developed his theory of gravity. Being open, curious, and unbiased at work paves the way for brand-new business models, technologies, and breakthrough ideas, from meal kits in a box delivered to your door, to Snapchat to ride sharing and space travel.

What possibilities could you unlock when you meet your own ideas and see the world around you unencumbered?

How: ·····································

1. **Get to know your biases.** Take a walk through the hallways at work and notice your inner chatter—the quick, brief labels and judgments that your mind is assigning to people, teams, spaces, and all that you encounter. Do you slightly move away from some people yet feel more comfortable with others? Feel more stress in certain rooms or situations?

2. **Check your mood.** Also pay attention to your emotional state. Is it positive or negative leaning? If the latter, take a break to reset. Go for a short walk; find a quiet place to do a five-minute practice of loving-kindness or taking in the good; or bring in the quality of gratitude by simply making a list of five things you are grateful for about your work.

3. **Release judgments.** As you acknowledge the limiting voices in your head throughout the day, do your best to suspend each one. Notice how your tendency to doubt or be cynical or favor certain people affects the narrative unfolding in your mind, and try extracting those attitudes for an unfiltered experience. This takes constant practice, but you'll become more and more adept at recognizing your ego versus possibility.

4. **Clear your mental whiteboard.** Maps (or mental models), best practices, and blueprints provide helpful shortcuts at work, but they can also limit the way you see things. Approach them with flexibility and curiosity, characteristics of a Beginner's Mind.

5. **Embrace curiosity.** As you practice being more receptive, ask questions, listen to ideas, and look for opportunities. Stretch your imagination without analyzing, criticizing, comparing, or minimizing the value of your thoughts. Welcome your Beginner's Mind. Give every idea (and every person) due consideration.

20

Banish multitasking

Increase productivity, flow, and enjoyment
by doing one thing at a time

· ·

"Anyone who can drive and kiss a girl is not giving the kiss the attention it deserves."

—Unknown

Hendrik was writing a research paper and a thought popped up: *I wonder what flights to Milan cost in May?* He clicked over to a travel website and started running some searches, and then went back to his writing. It took him a while to pick up his train of thought, and soon after he composed a few sentences, he considered checking whether an alternate city would be cheaper than Milan. And so it goes for so many of us.

Multitasking means you're doing more than one thing at the same time, such as writing a paper and searching the web, or talking on the phone while building a spreadsheet and drafting an email. Multitasking is the opposite of mindful focus: Many of us spend our days in a state of divided attention and constant toggling between activities, and it keeps us from truly being present. This will come as a shock to many, but your brain is *not* designed to multitask. Sure, you can have a conversation while walking or you can drink coffee while driving, but what your brain *cannot* do is really concentrate on two things at once.

Dr. Earl Miller, a neuroscientist at MIT and one of the world's foremost experts on divided attention, told *Inc.com* that "when people think they're multitasking, they're actually just switching from one task to another very rapidly. And every time they do, there's a cognitive cost." Although some feel as if they are getting more done when multitasking, studies show that up to 40 percent of productivity could be lost, which Miller refers to as a "switch cost." In an interview with *TIME* magazine, he observes, "Your brain stumbles a bit, and it requires time to get back to where it was before it was distracted. You're not able to think as deeply on something when you're being distracted every few minutes. And thinking deeply is where real insights come from."

Indeed, the science is persuasive. Neuroscientist Daniel J. Levitin explains in a Q&A with the *Guardian* that the shifting attention causes the prefrontal cortex (the part of the brain located just behind the forehead that controls abstract thinking and analysis and also helps you sustain attention) and the striatum (another part of the forebrain that plays a role in motivation and rewards) to burn through oxygenated glucose (aka blood sugar)—the same fuel that these brain regions need to stay focused on a task.

The rapid, continual shifts typical of multitasking can cause your brain to burn through fuel so quickly that you deplete its nutrients and feel exhausted, even after a short time. This state compromises your cognitive, emotional, and physical performance. In fact, some studies have found that when people are interrupted and splitting their attention, it takes them 50 percent longer to accomplish a task and they're much more likely to make errors. Worse yet, the ongoing lack of focus can lead to anxiety, which raises levels of the stress hormone cortisol, as well as adrenaline, which can cause mental fog and scrambled decision making. A 2015 Stanford study confirmed this, demonstrating that those who multitask are indeed worse performers, and those who "media multitask" (watching TV while cruising Instagram) cannot filter out irrelevant information when trying to complete goals.

But for me, the biggest drawback of multitasking is that it impedes creativity and "flow." Psychologist Mihaly Csikszentmihalyi, a leader in the field of positive psychology, was the first to coin the term "flow" in his pioneering book of the same name, published in 1990. Csikszentmihalyi writes that when you're in flow, you're completely absorbed in an activity—especially an activity where your abilities are matched to a challenge. He discovered that people find joy and satisfaction during this heightened state of consciousness. Flow is being consciously engaged with whatever you are doing. Csikszentmihalyi discovered that people find joy and satisfaction during this heightened state of consciousness. Csikszentmihalyi's contemporary, American psychologist Martin Seligman, explains in his book *Flourish* that consistently experiencing flow is associated with sustainable happiness and well-being. Athletes call it being in the "zone." The mindfulness coach to the NBA, George Mumford, says that mindfulness helps get you "flow ready."

Yet we get in our own way of flow when we start multitasking, and the addiction to it might go deeper than the drive to check off more items on our to-do lists. Habits are created with rewards, and multitasking not only gives the illusion of getting more accomplished, it also gives you a chemical hit that reinforces the habit. When you complete a small task like scheduling a meeting, returning an email, or making a call, a dose of dopamine (the brain's reward hormone) is released. And because your brain loves dopamine, it makes the allure of switching between quick tasks and getting more hits seem irresistible. Neuroscientists call this the dopamine-addiction feedback loop—when your brain rewards you for losing focus and looking for a new task. I call it brain candy.

But there's more: Your brain also has a bias for novelty. It can be easily distracted by a "shiny object," which for you might be a text from an old friend or a news alert from the *New York Times.* To top it off, attending to all of these shiny objects—saying yes to lunch with a friend, reading today's news, deleting an unwanted promotional email—makes you feel like you're getting things done. And you are, in a sense. But you're also sacrificing efficiency, productivity, and deep concentration.

You can offset this by setting a specific task to focus on, and then practicing resisting distractions. Remember that you can train your brain through repetition. Studies have shown, for example, that practicing mindful breathing meditation can strengthen your prefrontal cortex. That boost can help you avoid giving in to an impulse to do two things at once. So if you're working on a task and feel compelled to shoot a quick email or make a call, stop and take a breath instead. Notice your impulse, acknowledge it, and, if you can, jot down the task on your to-do list and get back to the work at hand. I like to use a timer to keep myself focused on a specific task for a set interval, and that structure removes any worry about checking the clock.

It's essential to also take deliberate planned breaks, and choose your distractions with thoughtfulness during that time. Instead of checking Facebook, opt to return an important personal phone call, make a dinner reservation for the family, or step outside and enjoy the fresh air. Be kind and understanding with your own biology. Knowing that you're hardwired to lose focus, to look for new sources of stimulation, and to seek rewards from dopamine hits can help you recognize what's temptation and what's truly important. Give sustained attention to your deserving priorities and you'll get higher-quality, greater creativity, and more time spent in the creative flow state. Meaningful accomplishment is your new reward.

How: ·

1. **Start with outcome.** Choose a single project to focus on, and get clear about what you intend to accomplish.

2. **Work in focused intervals.** Set a goal that is time-bound. Focus for 60 to 90 minutes, take a break, and then start another focus interval. Turn alerts off and put your phone five feet away.

3. **Catch yourself multitasking.** If you notice that your attention is divided between two tasks, great job already! Awareness is the first step to habit change. Choose the priority task, stop any others, and work sequentially, one thing at a time. Notice your impulse to jump to another activity, take a breath, and return attention to the task at hand.

4. **Take purposeful breaks.** Create a pause and nourish your mind and body with a healthy snack or getting outside. Let go of gadgets and take a walk in nature to reengage your default network that boosts creativity and gives your prefrontal cortex a break. Or allow yourself to daydream, doodle, or draw—activities that all have a similar effect.

5. **Try "Just Three Breaths."** Here is a mini-practice that might become a favorite, as it is for me. To help you pause when you catch yourself multitasking, take three slow breaths. With the first breath, focus on breathing to calm the mind, while saying, *"Calm."* On the second breath, relax the body, while saying, *"Relax."* On the third breath, focus your mind and heart by asking yourself *"What is most important now?"*

21

Face difficult emotions

*See emotions as separate from you and learn
to stay with them with kind attention.*

• •

"Why do you want to shut out of your life any uneasiness, any misery,
any depression, since after all you don't know what work these conditions are doing inside you?"

—Rainer Maria Rilke, poet, author

Whether we want to admit it or not, emotions impact our work.
Intense feelings like frustration, anger, and fear can undermine performance, block creativity, and harm professional relationships—especially when you aren't even aware of them. We're naturally inclined to
turn away from unpleasantness, which is why difficult emotions are
often left to bubble just under the radar. When we're working, dis-
tracting ourselves from our challenging emotions can be too easy: We
jump onto the next call, immerse ourselves in another project, or type
out another email.

When you don't recognize and allow emotions as they occur, however,
it can cost you. Suppressed emotions can affect your health, your relationships, and your results. Often, they "leak out" in the form of lashing out
when you least expect it—as rash behaviors or hurtful barbs. Or, for some

people, suppressed feelings can lead to withdrawal, silence, and isolation.

But one of the most useful aspects of mindfulness is a shift in how we understand and relate to our emotions. What if I told you that your unpleasant emotions are like the fleeting pain of a stubbed toe: sensations that move through the body with a beginning, middle, and end? If you're like me, you might find this idea of transience liberating, knowing that the negative feeling will pass.

The physical, short-lived pain of a stubbed toe isn't just a metaphor. Emotions begin in the body as a physiological response to some stimulus—an event, interaction, or anything happening around you, or even within. Mindfulness expands your ability to notice the early indicators of emotions, like your stomach clenching, warmth in your cheeks, or dryness in your mouth. Although most of us in Western cultures "live in our head," you can increase your ability to sense these early signals with the body scan practice. In effect, as you train with the body scan you give a workout to your insula—the part of the brain associated with detecting physiological sensations. And with repetition, you become more adept at *interoception,* your capacity to sense with more detail and vividness the information that your body is giving you.

One of the benefits of this emotional awareness is catching your body's signals just as they begin to arise—perhaps before you are even cognitively aware that they are there. These initial signals serve as your "early warning system," cluing you in to the wisdom of your body. You become more masterly at managing emotions when you more aware—and aware sooner. Emotions steer your actions—so tuning in to them before they hijack your behavior (whether it's running away or making regretful remarks) is that much more important. With interoception, the physicality of emotions can feel concrete instead of overwhelming and abstract. The same is true with understanding that they are phenomena simply passing through us. A metaphor that my clients find useful is the Big Sky Mind. Think of yourself as a vast, blue sky, and of your emotions as clouds that come and go. You—your awareness, your consciousness—are always there. But the rest, as Buddhist teacher and author Pema Chödrön says, is just the weather.

The mindfulness quality of impermanence is at play here. Whether the emotion is difficult (like sadness) or easy (like happiness), you become less attached to it when you see it as a temporary phenomenon, rather than a permanent character trait. For many, that's a pretty powerful reframe. Consider the difference between the thoughts *I am angry* and *Anger is here. I am sad* or *I am angry* is language that seems to wrap us up inside the emotion: We overidentify it. Saying *anger or sadness is here* or *is present right now* emphasizes the fleeting, impermanent nature of emotions and gives you the capacity of equanimity, a spacious, less reactive freedom to choose how to respond. It reaffirms that your emotions are variable but you are not.

Emotional regulation gets easier with practice. As you learn to identify emotions, understanding them as something separate from yourself, you can also learn to allow emotions to arise and pass, instead of reacting impulsively out of old habits—whether it's numbing out, raiding the office snack machine, or logging in to Facebook. This is known to some as "learning to stay"—accepting your emotions without judgment, blame, or shame, and letting them flow through you.

Consciousness of and openness to emotions—no matter if they are pleasant or unpleasant—helps you regulate your response, rather than letting the feelings whip you around. The point is to get familiar with recognizing emotions in the body, and not try to suppress them. This way, you can handle your emotions with perspective and kindness: There I go—my face is flushing and I'm feeling nervous. It's far less taxing to experience an unpleasant feeling when you see what's happening. Emotional awareness and acceptance can be the difference between being upset over a conversation for 10 minutes and being upset all day. Neuroscientist Richard Davidson describes this as increasing our resilience—the rapidity at which we recover from adversity—whether it is a difficult emotion or a major life event.

Sometimes, though, our emotions feel more consuming than constructive, and there are tools that can help. Mental noting (different from labeling) is one such skill. Neuropsychiatrist Dan Siegel describes how detecting and naming emotions can be a way to build self-control and stability. When you use words to describe your internal emotional states, you shift activity from the emotional (limbic) part of your brain to the rational, thinking center in your brain (the prefrontal cortex), which is the center for executive functioning. That means you are more capable of regulating emotions in an adaptive, flexible way. I used to teach my young daughter to "use her words" when she was upset. A similar mantra is "name it to tame it."

Katherine, a magazine editor in New York City and one of my corporate clients, put this ability to use in a critical meeting with the publication's circulation team. Katherine noticed her throat clench and heat rise to her face. Thanks to her months of mindful breathing and body scan practice, she recognized the sensations: *Worry is here. I am sensing fear in my body.* Katherine breathed deeply and observed the emotions as they moved like waves; she did not try to ignore them, change the topic, or leave the room. Instead she asked herself what was going on—what was she telling herself? Soon she realized that she was afraid of the repeatedly diminishing circulation numbers and the impact that they would have on her quarterly results. Acknowledging this brought Katherine's rational brain back online and helped her calm her nervous system, using the emotional response as informative data. As she took deep breaths, she found herself able to see with greater resolution, to accept her fear, and to start generating creative solutions from a clearer mind.

Like the weather, emotions are always changing, gradually becoming something else. And body signals are your own "check engine light," drawing your attention and giving you important information that enables you to regulate and adapt. In this sense, mindfulness will serve you as a professional—and in every other role that you assume in life. I find the words of teacher and author James Baraz to be a great reminder of this principle: "Mindfulness is simply being aware of what is happening right now without wishing it were different; enjoying the pleasant without holding on when it changes (which it will); being with the unpleasant without fearing it will always be this way (which it won't)."

How:

1. **Recognize.** This is the first step in a helpful acronym for dealing with difficult emotions (RAIN) that I learned from Tara Brach, founder of the Insight Meditation Community in Washington, D.C., and one of my main teachers. The RAIN practice starts with noticing (recognizing) how you feel and taking a few easy breaths. As the emotion arises, you might sense changes in your stomach, your throat, your face—heat, tension, tightness. Try to name the emotion with loving awareness: Oh, okay, anxious.

2. **Allow.** Don't run from the emotion, suppress it, or turn to distraction or a habitual, comforting refuge like food, alcohol, or the Internet. Don't judge or blame—yourself or others. The pause of recognition and acceptance allows the feelings to simply be there while you deepen your attention.

3. **Investigate with kindness.** Use inquiry to uncover what is happening. Ask yourself: What is this like? What am I feeling right now? Where is this most noticeable in my body? What needs my attention? Describe and name what is there. Sadness in my abdomen. My throat is clenched, I am feeling attacked. Excitement in my chest. My cheeks are hot, I am feeling embarrassed—I am reacting to my boss's public admonishment, and worried about my reputation.

4. **Nurture.** Attend and befriend your feelings. You can use a physical gesture such as placing your hand on your heart, or you can simply pause and breathe for a moment of recognition, acceptance, and self-compassion. Self-compassion is soothing, so send an inward message of kindness, such as *I know this a hard moment. Many people experience this at work. May you be at ease. May you be peaceful.*

22

Create space when overwhelmed

*Regular moments of "mental white space" reduce
the anxiety of feeling overwhelmed*

. . . .

"Between stimulus and response there is a space. In that space lies our
freedom and our power to choose our response. In our response lies our
growth and our freedom."

—Stephen Covey, describing the teachings of Viktor Frankl

In her book *Overwhelmed,* journalist Brigid Schulte chronicles the current
epidemic in Western cultures of feeling overwhelmed, overworked, and
overtired. I immediately related to her book; at times I feel like there
aren't enough hours in the day to meet all my work commitments and
still have time for play, running a home, and caring for myself and my
family. Perhaps you feel the same way at times.

But what are the drivers of overwhelm? Although the norms in our
society and organization cultures certainly contribute to the epidemic—
leaner teams, expectations of being "always-on," ever present, and connected 24/7—many of the factors that contribute to overwhelm come
from within. Mindfulness helps cultivate self-awareness. When you pay

attention to the sensation of being overwhelmed, you can investigate the causes and start to shift the patterns. For example, sometimes our own beliefs about how much we have to take on, what we have to say yes to, and what "done" looks like contribute to the workload on our desk. Without awareness, you can keep repeating the patterns that create the hamster wheel, as well as the habitual ways you respond when you feel like projects and demands are just too much to manage.

One of the causes of overwhelm is that we simply lose focus on what really matters. During the workweek, you might be swamped with project deadlines, meetings, Skype calls, and unread emails—in addition to personal commitments. This was true for an attorney I was coaching, who often felt besieged by the pressures of her law firm. She described her typical day to me: "Most often I just jump into whatever email has come in, or I take every call that's put through, or do whatever feels most pressing. I want to get it done and off my plate." Like her, you might notice a similar impulse to act on what is urgent rather than what's really important. But you can create space between the impulse and the action. Step back from what you're doing and take three mindful breaths. Then think about what you were working on. By breathing, you give yourself a window to reconnect to your intentions, values, purpose, daily plan, and weekly goals. Is the interruption a higher priority or simply a distraction from your current task? Choose to reset and refocus your attention and energy on what matters most.

Where do your energy and time go, and why? Many of us tend to unwittingly spend much of our energy on low-priority activities compared to high-value activities to meet a balanced set of needs such as physical, mental, emotional, spiritual, and relational, for example. But remember that being busy does not necessarily mean being effective.

Another consideration with managing our day is that we often overestimate how much we can get done, and underestimate how much time each activity will take. Try doing a time audit on yourself for a few days, either by journaling or using an app that records time spent. As you observe how you spend your day, ask yourself, *Where is my time going and why? Am I overestimating how much I can get done and underestimat-*

ing what it takes to do it? Can I add buffers in my schedule to allow for that tendency?

Also, as your self-awareness grows, notice what you believe about asking for help, delegating, setting boundaries, and saying "no." Journaling can help here—at the end of the day, reflect on what you would do differently or adjust in your self-management beliefs, assumptions, and habits. Also jot down what went well that day, and your role in making it happen.

Many of us power through projects alone, reluctant to pull in others even when needed. I know this from firsthand experience. In the early days of PurposeBlue, when the business started rapidly growing, I resisted expanding my team too quickly and instead took on more and more work. It took mindful awareness to recognize my resistance and fears around growing too fast, and then I was able to increase the team. I also had to see I had competing goals (growth and effectiveness), and it was hard to say "no" to new projects or clients. Now when I receive a request, I take time and space before I respond. I check in with my body, asking how this prospective opportunity makes me feel—energized and light or unmotivated and heavy? And I check in with my purpose: Does the project align with my values and purpose? Is the client or business a good fit for the work we want to do and who we want to serve?

Recall the quote from Viktor Frankl's teachings about the space between stimulus and response. It's about shifting from compulsion to choice, making room to breathe, reflect, and act with skill. Next time you sense yourself becoming overwhelmed or anxious, stop and take three deep breaths—or what's sometimes known as the "sacred pause." The space you create gives rise to your own inner wisdom, and a chance to reconnect with what matters. Then you can decide how to respond.

Most people are living a good chunk of their day unconsciously—rushing from task to task, saying yes more than no, not aligning energy and time with what matters most. Becoming more conscious about how you spend your energy and resources will help with reducing overwhelm as you let go of habits, people, and activities that drain your energy. Experiment with strategies to create mental space during overwhelm with the sacred pause, three breaths to focus, or the STOP practice that follows.

Practice the sacred pause, and get familiar with your default patterns. When you're overwhelmed, do you find that you work faster, put in longer hours, or just check out entirely? Understanding your tendencies can help you increase your resilience during times of overwhelm and create space when those moments do show up. You can choose the actions that best serve you, your company, and the people you care about.

How: ·

1. **Stop.** Simply stop. This is the hardest part, but it's also the most important because it is the one that creates space. Practice awareness and recognition of what overwhelm feels like in your body, thoughts, feelings, and behaviors. You might notice tightness in your throat or chest, that your speech speeds up or that you interrupt others, you are feeling impatient, or you have thoughts of limitation, not enough or lack of time. As you become aware that the stress of overwhelm is present, take time to pause.

2. **Take three breaths.** Direct your attention away from your spinning thoughts and feelings and toward your breath to calm and relax both mind and body with slow, easy breaths. You can count to 10 if three is not enough.

3. **Observe and inquire.** Take stock of your direct experience by guiding attention inward. What are you sensing in your body? What are you thinking? Are you judging or blaming yourself or others for the situation? Is your inner critic louder than usual? Inquire with an attitude of kindness and care, as you would if you were supporting an overwhelmed friend.

4. **Proceed with skillful next steps.** What actions can you take to care for yourself and move forward toward what matters most? Could you take a walk and then come back to your highest-priority project? Could you ask your boss for help, or negotiate a new deadline? Talk to yourself with kindness as you determine your next best action.

23

Prepare for a tough conversation

*Bring awareness to the issues at the root
of difficult conversations*

. . . .

"Remember then: there is only one time that is important—Now!
It is the most important time because it is the only time when we
have any power."

—Leo Tolstoy, author

Have you ever said "yes" when you meant "no"? Avoided a conversation
that you knew you needed to have? Or have you had a tough conversation that didn't go well—meaning the person never came around to
seeing that you were right? Whether you are negotiating with a client,
dealing with an underperforming employee, or asking for a raise, it can
be hard to actively choose to have a difficult conversation. Humans are
hardwired to steer clear of discomfort; we'd much rather seek pleasure
and move away from pain. Having a hard conversation is categorically
in the "pain" bucket because it might mean stepping into an unresolved
issue, an ongoing disagreement, a pending negotiation, or an incident
that felt unfair or disappointing. And, unfortunately, this natural

aversion to discomfort can prevent connection and resolution where it is needed most.

As you train in mindfulness, you strengthen the very qualities and skills that can help you achieve the outcomes you hope for at work, especially in the midst of difficulty. Having a hard conversation can help to clear up a misunderstanding, repair a wrong, rebuild trust, and lay the foundation for collaboration. Mindfulness facilitates these outcomes by developing your ability to see what is happening at a "meta-level"—as if you were a spectator of your own life. William Ury, co-author of the best-selling *Getting to Yes,* describes it as getting to the balcony, as if you're watching a situation unfold like a play on a stage. When you are meta-aware, you can strengthen your capacity to shift into an observer perspective and see what is happening—or, in some cases, not happening. With meta-awareness, you can notice when you are avoiding a conversation that actually has the potential to get you a better outcome.

When you're on autopilot, rushing from meeting to meeting and phone call to phone call, it's easy to lose sight of the bigger picture. In our desire to avoid confrontation, we can ignore or repress signals—both internal and external—that something is wrong. Or, we can become so entrenched in our thoughts, tasks, and busyness that we don't consider the experience of those around us, or we lose sight of overarching values and goals. Sensing these signals with mindful awareness can help you realize when a conversation is needed so you can more masterfully navigate the relationship.

Taking time to prepare gives you courage to face the unpleasant and ease the fear that often looms in advance of a tough conversation, and the first step is to recognize that these types of exchanges go beyond words. Researchers at the Harvard Negotiation Project suggest bringing attention to three layers:

- Content (what happened, that is, the objective facts)
- Feelings (what emotions are present in this situation)
- Questions of identity (how you view yourself)

Within that last layer of identity are underlying questions that can reveal what is really at the core of the difficulty:

- *Am I competent? (Do I have what it takes?)*
- *Am I a good person?*
- *Am I worthy of love and respect?*

Being human means that there are *always* identity issues at the core. Consider a manager who keeps checking on the status of a project that a direct report is running. The project isn't due for two months, but the team member is starting to resent what feels like a micromanaging boss. The team member might think: *Does my manager think I can pull this off* (competence)? *Does he or she think I will blow this off* (good person)? *Does he or she appreciate the autonomy of my role?* When you bring light to the deeper driving forces that are linked to identity, you can open your mind and your heart—essential to forging effective relationships, and building strong teams and powerful partnerships.

Explore these layers one by one before treading into delicate territory. Consider what's beneath the surface for you *and* for the other person. Try to understand and acknowledge intent and impact. Denying or defending your own impact can be more destructive than the initial event that caused the conflict. But try to evaluate others by their intention versus their impact. Did they intend to disrespect you or diminish your autonomy? Recognizing the greater forces at work can help you shift from a constricted way of being—attached to your position—to an expanded understanding and ability to cultivate compassion for yourself and the other person.

Difficult conversations are necessary and not easy. They require that you face what you would rather avoid, that you open yourself up to working with strong emotions, and that you take time to look deeply at what is going on with yourself and others instead of quickly jumping to a resolution. By practicing mindfulness, you are already learning to let go of judgments and biases so that receptivity, curiosity, and compassion can guide you. It takes courage and vulnerability, but you lay the groundwork for understanding, and hopefully, peace.

How: •••

1. **Aim to go beneath the surface.** Beyond the context and the content of what happened, start with the intention to look deeply at the situation with curiosity.

2. **Enlist a sounding board.** Ask a colleague or friend to listen while you go through both sides. If you don't have another person, journal each side of the story.

3. **Explore all perspectives.** Bring empathy to both sides of the situation. Walk through content, feelings, and identity from your point of view and then from the other person's point of view with your chosen colleague or friend. *What is at stake for them? What might their intention be?*

4. **Decide next steps.** Sometimes just talking through both sides is enough. Determine if you still need a conversation.

5. **Invite the other person to talk first.** Do your best mindful listening. Practice the mindful qualities of acceptance and compassion as you explore perspectives together.

24

Reframe challenging situations

*When the mind is calm and clear, you can
shift perspectives for wise perception*

• •

**"When you change the way you look at things, the things you look
at change."**

—Max Planck, German theoretical physicist,
winner of the 1918 Nobel Prize

You lose funding for a major project. A top client is upset. Your right-
hand person quits. You lose a competitive bid. Challenging situations are
a part of being human and a seemingly never-ending part of the work
environment. Mindfulness cannot erase or prevent slipups altogether.
But building your capacity for mindfulness means being able to notice,
accept, and allow the messiness, without arguing, fighting, or wishing it
away. If you can open up to the difficulty as a fundamental part of life
and realize that it's okay, you can explore it with less resistance and,
therefore, less suffering. Here's a well-known mindfulness formula that
captures this point:

Suffering = Pain × Resistance

Suffering represents your emotional distress and discomfort. Pain, in this scenario, is the challenging situation—you missed a major deadline due to a major misunderstanding or make a serious programming error costing the company a fortune, for example. Thus emotional stress and difficulty come from the degree to which you resist the situation, which might look like denying, fighting, or wishing it were different. So although a painful or challenging situation might be out of your control, the degree to which you mentally resist it is in your control, ultimately increasing how hard things are and the suffering you experience because of it.

Stress works this way. Stress is not a "thing" that happens; it's your body's response to the meaning you assign to what is happening. Let's say you hear that your company is being acquired and your job is on the line. How you appraise or relate to this "stressor" will ultimately determine your reaction. Fear, anger, or confusion can trigger your neurobiological stress response, releasing chemicals that not only affect your body, but also your thinking. Perceived threats are stressors that direct blood flow away from the cognitive part of the brain and into the limbs, and narrow your view to focus on the "danger," a survival instinct from evolutionary biology. This was helpful when our ancestors were escaping predators, but today you need more than fight, flight, or freeze. You need a strategy to get calm and restore broader perspective.

That comes from your explanatory style: how your powerful meaning-making mind evaluates whatever is happening in your life. As with strong emotions, your bodily response can help you recognize symptoms of stress—headaches, stomach pains, a rapid heartbeat are all common signals. Next time you're experiencing this, notice what's going on (maybe you missed an important meeting) and what you are telling yourself (perhaps in your absence, you think you'll be perceived as a less important part of the team, or as forgetful or incompetent).

Psychologist Kelly McGonigal's research on stress reduction suggests that your *view* of stress impacts your health far more than the stressor itself. "The harmful effects of stress on health are not inevitable," McGonigal said in a TED talk that she gave in 2013. "How you think and how you act can transform your experience of stress. When you choose to view your stress response as helpful, you create the biology of courage. And when you choose to connect with others under stress, you can create resilience." Are those sweaty palms before pitching a new client signaling that you should be nervous and worried, or can you view it as your body mobilizing into action?

As you practice reflecting on your own tendencies, you might discover certain "mindsets" that you hold. Stanford professor Carol Dweck defines a mindset as a mental frame or lens that selectively organizes and encodes information, thereby orienting you toward a unique way of understanding an experience and guiding you toward certain actions and responses. In her best-selling book *Mindset,* Dweck finds that people with a "growth mindset" interpret their strengths and talents as variable (changeable with effort), while people with a "fixed mindset" see their traits as invariable and permanent.

People with a fixed mindset avoid risks, challenges, and failures, because it threatens their very sense of identity—*I'm smart and I failed* can become *I thought I was smart, but I failed.* A growth mindset, on the other hand, will see a situation of failure or not quite getting it as a learning opportunity: *This was hard and I can't do it yet, but I am learning.* "Yet" is a key word to adopt, becoming more conscious of how you interpret challenges and setbacks, and how you can stretch goals. A growth mindset infuses you with energy and aspiration to take things on. It might not be your default reaction yet, but the more you practice self-awareness and reframing, the more easily a positive, growth mindset—the response that follows—will come.

How: •••

1. **Recognize your body's signals.** When you sense your body tightening up, heart pounding, chest feeling heavy, take a mindful pause—just notice what you're experiencing right then, without suppressing it or pushing it away.

2. **Settle your mind and body.** Take three breaths and allow your mind and body to calm, so the rational, thinking part of your brain can operate with clarity. In some cases, counting to 10 is what helps most.

3. **Accept life as it is.** See situations just as they are, accepting that some things are within your ability to influence and change, whereas others must just be accepted and allowed.

4. **Take a wider perspective.** Consider a stressful situation from many angles, including an empathetic view of what is at stake for others, and a positive perspective of what good might come.

5. **Adopt a growth mindset.** View the difficult situation as impermanent, and see yourself as an adaptable learner, who will become more agile, wise, and resilient through every challenge.

25

Calm your inner critic

Embrace the voice in your head with objectivity and compassion

. . . .

"Meditation . . . what it really does is change your relationship to the voice in your head."

—Dan Harris, ABC News anchor

If you could listen to the voice in my head during a typical workday, you might hear:

Stay focused, you are distracted. Don't forget to update the coaching contract for Jon. I am not going to get the proposal developed on time. I forgot to pick up the vacationing neighbor's mail. Is the orthodontist appointment this week or next? Oops—nothing in the house for dinner again.

We spend much of our lives governed by the voice in our head. The nonstop, inner chatter is constantly running—the insatiable wanting, comparing, evaluating, reacting to our experiences, and the unending self-referential thinking. And it is often harsh. In our culture, the unwritten message is that being hard on yourself is the price you have to pay to get things done, and meet the often impossible expectations, standards, and ideals we sometimes hold for ourselves.

But according to Dr. Kristin Neff, a leading researcher on self-compassion and associate professor in human development at the

University of Texas at Austin, self-criticism only sabotages you and produces a variety of negative consequences. Research suggests that self-criticism can lead to lowered self-esteem, anxiety, and depression. Self-compassion, on the other hand, has been found to be empowering and motivating. It's a loving act you do for yourself, one that Neff defines as having three components:

1. Mindfulness—being aware of but not "overidentified" with mental or emotional phenomena, or simply recognizing that you are in a difficult moment or hearing your harsh inner voice
2. Common humanity—recognizing that suffering, setbacks, and failure are part of the shared human experience, versus the idea that "there's something wrong with me"
3. Self-kindness—meeting oneself with warmth and kindness, rather than harmful self-criticism or judgment

Yet people seem to resist a self-compassionate approach for myriad reasons: Some see it as "soft," or believe that an attitude of acceptance will lead to avoidance of problems or lack of motivation. Some fear that self-kindness could make us passive about our own or others' ethical missteps. But research has shown the opposite to be true. A fascinating 2012 study at the University of California, Berkeley asked if treating oneself with self-compassion after making a mistake could lead to self-improvement. Researchers trained participants in two control groups to view setbacks or failures as ways to enhance either self-compassion or self-esteem; for a third control group, they gave no guidance. In their responses, the self-compassion participants were the most likely to see their weaknesses as changeable, and to be more motivated to improve and avoid the same mistake in the future (they spent significantly more time studying for the second round of a test on which they had previously received low scores). The results suggest that self-compassion is more effective than criticism *and* more effective than a self-esteem boost not only in helping you cope with a setback, but also in encouraging you to move forward.

If self-compassion feels counterintuitive to your current tendencies, know that you can shift how you see and relate to the voice in your head. Here's an example of what it looks like:

Jennifer, a media photographer in Washington, D.C., and a mindfulness coaching client of mine, had a hard time taming the admonishing commentary in her head, and she believed that it was necessary for her to excel—in fact, she attributed her success to it. Jennifer feared that if she changed how she talked to herself, she wouldn't be able to juggle all the balls in the air and get her projects over the finish line. I coached her to start paying attention to her internal negative comments, phrases like: *You should have . . . You are always . . .* and learn to hear herself with kind understanding . . . *I hear you, I know you are worried, thank you,* as if she were recasting the inner critic as an inner protector.

Jennifer noticed a change. She began to talk to herself with compassion instead of judgment or criticism. She practiced the three steps of self-compassion with phrases like:

This is a tough moment/day/week. This assignment is very challenging. (mindfulness)

Many people are going through this today. This is part of being human. (common humanity)

May you be at ease, happy, and well. May you receive the help you need. (self-kindness)

Recently, I taught the self-kindness phrase *It's okay, sweetheart* to a group of 120 men and women from across Europe that had gathered in Paris. Since then, I have received emails from both genders telling me how much this one line has transformed how they talk to themselves, and how they can shift their internal state with the three steps of self-compassion. Jennifer shared that she has had more confidence in facing challenges during what has been a tough year. With practice, she honed her ability to hear her judging voice, and the connection to a larger common humanity brings her unexpected relief; she doesn't feel as alone or isolated in the experience. The biggest boost came in learning how to direct loving-kindness to herself through a compassionate response to tough moments. Imagine speaking to and supporting yourself as you would a loved one, and the possibilities that can come when you turn kindness inward.

How: ·

1. **Deepen your self-awareness.** Pay attention to the language you use to talk to yourself. Would you say that to a friend?

2. **Make friends with the voice in your head.** Realize that the worrying, scolding voice is trying to help you, keep you out of trouble, and be sure you're okay. Greet the voice with, *Thank you. I know you are trying to help. I am okay. I've got this.*

3. **Realize that you are not alone.** Everyone struggles. Realizing that you are not the only one to fail, experience job loss, drop the ball, hurt others, or make mistakes helps you see that all of this is part of being human.

4. **Have mindful loving-kindness phrases ready.** When you think, *I blew it* or *You can't do this,* you can say the following phrases and offer yourself compassion:
   - *This is a difficult moment.*
   - *Many people experience this. I am not alone.*
   - *May I be kind to myself. May I give myself what I need. May I be strong.*

5. **Use a gesture.** Try deepening this self-compassion practice with a gesture, by putting your hand on your heart or holding your forearm—whatever feels comfortable—while you say the phrases. Gentle physical touch can immediately create a soothing effect on your body's nervous system, release oxytocin, and quiet the voice within.

26

End the work day
with ease

*Establish a mindful routine for closing the day
with acceptance, letting go, and gratitude*

. . . .

"When [your mind calms], there's room to hear more subtle things—
that's when your intuition starts to blossom and you start to see things
more clearly."

—Steve Jobs, former CEO of Apple

The end of the workday is fertile ground for cultivating mindfulness. You
can complete your workday with awareness and intention, or you can
end it by multitasking and bolting through the doorway. The decision
seems obvious, but it's not always easy to execute.

Many of my clients have adopted a practice of setting aside 20 minutes
before they leave work to close the day in a more mindful way, integrating
reflection, acceptance, and gratitude. Sound impossible? Try to build this
into your day by scheduling a daily meeting with yourself at 5:00 p.m.
or before you generally start to wrap up.

Use this time for reflection on what went well and what got in the
way. Self-awareness deepens as you practice inquiring about your work

habits and common distractions. Is there a time of day or are there certain events that you most often associate with losing focus? What can you do differently to "hack" those traps going forward? Can you accept the parts of the day that didn't go as planned or were unpleasant surprises? Follow this acceptance practice by letting go with peace, knowing that tomorrow is another day. Leave these elements of the day behind when you close the laptop, or clean the paint brushes, and walk out the door.

Next, reflect on what contributed to things working well, a practice that positive psychologist Martin Seligman advocates. Did you listen to a meditation on the way to work? Did you run or participate in a mindful meeting? Did you begin the day with clear intentions and stay focused for the most part? Remember: There's no judgment—just an open mind, acceptance, and kindness. Becoming more conscious of how you choose to spend your time, connect with others, and do your work promotes learning and growth, and as the philosopher Seneca advised, makes the most of your days right now.

Finally, wrap up with a moment of grateful appreciation, a quality that can amplify all aspects of your life. Review your day through a lens of thankfulness—for a new customer, a smile you got from a colleague in the hall, the surprise invitation to lunch, the presentation you knocked out of the ballpark—and write down three things in your journal, on a notepad, or in an app. A powerful next question to ask yourself is:

- *How did the things you're grateful for come about?*
- *What was your role in making it happen?*

According to Seligman in his book *Flourish,* this simple thought process activates a positive state of mind and expands your appreciation for the interconnection in life and your own agency in generating the good.

Whether it's for a total of five minutes or 15, pausing at the end of your workday and practicing acceptance, letting go, and gratitude sets you up to move into the next part of your day with a centered, clear, presence.

How:

1. **Honor the time.** Decide how much time to protect for ending the day peacefully. Set up your recurring meeting to end the day with ease and stick to it.

2. **Start with three breaths.** By now you're getting the hang of this: Begin almost any mindfulness practice by focusing on the breath, relaxing the body, and stepping into the present moment, to whatever is important right now.

3. **Check in with your state.** Notice how you're doing. Do you have emotion bottled up from an earlier meeting? Excitement about a new project or investment? Recognize what's there, and allow it to be there versus suppressing or denying it.

4. **Reflect on the day.** Note where you made progress on meaningful work or reflect on what got in the way with nonjudgmental attention. Accept how the day went, and let go of any lingering emotions, regrets, or "should haves." Take a few minutes to write down what you're grateful for on this particular day, or mentally savor the good—appreciating your results, connections with people, and contributions made. Delight in your accomplishments.

5. **Set intentions and plan for the next day.** Turn attention to your commitments. Jot down three things that are most important to do tomorrow. This step frees your mind from ruminating on them, and gives you a clear jumping-off point when you get to work the next day.

Play:
Enjoy the Day

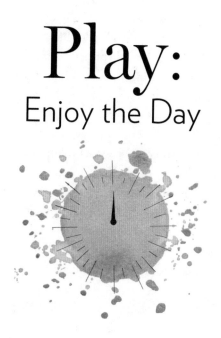

Children play—they explore, imagine, enact, create, run, jump, and laugh. It is the universal language of childhood. You don't have to tell them to play; they just do it naturally. As adults, we tend to play less and less in our busy lives. Whether you enjoy a tennis match with a friend, throwing a Frisbee, flying down a ski slope, or letting loose in a spontaneous dance party, you can pay attention to how you use your leisure time—and how present you are when you do so—to increase your happiness.

Why does play matter? In his book *Play: How It Shapes the Brain, Opens the Imagination, and Invigorates the Soul,* psychiatrist Dr. Stuart Brown describes the significance of play in the lives of animals and humans. With the support of the National Geographic Society and anthropologist Jane Goodall, Brown studied animal play in the wild.

He discovered that play is an evolved behavior important for the well-being—not to mention the survival—of animals, especially those of higher intelligence. Well-being does not come from a fleeting emotion or a temporary pleasant experience. It is an optimal state of being that comes from being engaged with your life, when you are realizing your full potential across mental, physical, spiritual, and relational dimensions, and contributing to something greater than yourself. Understanding that play is a key ingredient of well-being elevates it from the enjoyable to the essential.

Leisure is the time we carve out for play, and a gateway to happiness. According to positive psychologist Sonja Lyubomirsky, up to 40 percent of happiness is affected by our behaviors: how we think and act every day. (The rest of our happiness is a mix of genetics and life circumstances.) That gives us a significant amount of control over our well-being, and makes our intentional activities—what we choose to do in our free time—all the more important. Mindfulness in *what* we do and *how* we do it can help us delight fully in good moments and create a life of more joy.

What I've noticed living in the United States, Germany, and Brazil is that people who know how to best enjoy their leisure time are the happiest. I know I still don't get enough play. My intention is to spend more time skiing, swimming, dancing, painting, and laughing with others. Do you have enough play in your life? Understanding how leisure contributes to well-being and joy is just one more reason to take it seriously. I encourage you to make play a priority—one that benefits you and the people you care about. In the following entries, I share my favorite strategies for using mindfulness to get the most out of the day and my quality time with others—and to grow the happiness that belongs in every day of our lives.

27

Take pictures

Your camera can be a handy tool to appreciate beauty and joy in the here and now

. . . .

"I am not interested in shooting new things—I am interested to see things new."

—Ernst Haas, **photographer**

In Tibet, the word *miksang* means "good eye." The "good" refers to your world and the idea that it is inherently rich and vivid just as it is. The "eye" refers to the practice of seeing—and comprehending this circumstance. Beauty is available all around us in everyday life when we are present. The moment of seeing what lives around us is the essence of paying attention on purpose—and a photograph can harvest the exquisite moment between what you observe and the wonder and joy that it can generate within you. Hunt for beauty like a child looking for seashells on the beach, and seek beauty in unexpected places, like on the face of a person in the very beginning of life, or near the end. With a camera in your hand, use a wider lens when you consider what is beautiful; go beyond "pretty" or "nice." Let yourself be surprised by how prevalent beauty is when you stop and look. A camera can help you do that.

Today, photography has become ubiquitous, thanks to the advancement in smartphones, tablets, and cameras themselves. A camera is a convenient tool to focus your attention and synchronize your mind and body, in what is called coherence, to a single moment of focus. Neurobiologist Daniel Siegel speaks often on the enormous upside to well-being when you can foster coherence in the moment. Taking pictures as well as looking at inspiring photos can be a joyful activity to integrate mindfulness into your leisure time.

But doesn't taking pictures take you *out* of being present? One of my clients told me about a wedding he attended. In the marriage program, the couple had printed the line, *Put your cameras down and just be here.* Although there are certainly times when one should put away technology and pay full attention, it is a common misperception that taking photos prevents people from being present. In fact, new research finds that most people who take photographs with attention actually enhance their appreciation for their experiences. The key is awareness: knowing whether the camera is causing you to miss out or is deepening engagement.

In a 2016 study published in the *Journal of Personality and Social Psychology,* Kristin Diehl and her team put participants on a real-life bus tour. Some were allowed to take photographs during the tour, and others were not. When surveyed, those who took photos said they enjoyed the experience significantly more than those who did not. In a similar study, Diehl's researchers found that participants who took photos of a restaurant meal enjoyed it significantly more than those who did not. In both studies, the researchers concluded that taking pictures increases engagement by directing greater visual attention to qualities of the experience that make you want to photograph it in the first place. Interestingly, the same is true for photography in situations that aren't pleasant or easy; taking photos results in worse evaluations of negative experiences.

In addition to enhancing attention and awareness, taking pictures (of pleasant situations!) can help promote positivity, gratitude, and joy. In a 2016 study from the University of California, researchers found that regularly snapping selfies and other images with a smartphone and sharing them with friends can improve a person's mindset. Participants taking selfies reported becoming more confident and comfortable; those taking photos of objects that made them happy became more appreciative; and those who took photos to make others happy became calmer and reported that the connection to family and friends reduced stress.

You can enjoy your own photos or drink in the supply of curated images now available on social media sites like Instagram to access joy, cultivate compassion, and inspire wonder. When a photo appears in my feed—be it a stunning glimpse of orange autumn trees, an image of a child in Flint, Michigan, suffering from lead poisoning, or a member of the Kulung tribe hunting honey while suspended from a mountainside in Nepal—I stop and pause. My perspective widens, I connect to the broader world, and I deepen my awareness of moments of happiness and moments of suffering that are occurring everywhere.

So wherever you are, simply keeping a camera handy can create opportunities to practice mindfulness—not only to sharpen the way you see the world, but also to amplify your feelings about what you are taking in.

How: •

1. **Plan a photography outing.** Whether for 15 minutes or a whole day, begin with the intention to see and capture beauty using your camera.
2. **Align intention with attention by picking a theme.** Choose an area of focus as you photograph, such as shadows, angles, movement, nature, perspective, a specific person, or a certain color.
3. **Practice letting go.** The phone application Snapchat allows you to take a photo, enjoy the moment, and let it go as it disappears later that day. You get the joy of capturing the image, and even sharing it, while also honing the qualities of impermanence and letting go: understanding that everything changes, and you don't have to cling to it.
4. **Combine photos and journaling.** Over the course of a week, take 10 photos of what matters most to you. At the end of the week, look at each photo and journal the answer to these questions: *What does this photo*

show? Why is this photo meaningful to me? By reflecting on the photos and your insights, you deepen engagement. Tumblr, VSCO, and Day One are apps that combine taking photos and journaling.

5. **Snap and share.** Take selfies with loved ones and then send the photos to others to give them a happiness jolt as well. When taking pictures, sharing, or posting, stop and pause, checking in on your intention and rejoicing in the beauty, joy, and connection that photography can create.

6. **Curate a gratitude wall.** Send favorite photos from a mobile phone to an online app like Mixtiles; a set of mounted images of what is most meaningful to you will be mailed right to your doorstep. Create a photographic gratitude and meaning wall that gives you a boost when you walk by. (Or print out the images on your printer and mount them yourself.)

28

Use music

*Music can train attention and awareness,
shift your mood, and unleash joy*

• •

**"The theory of relativity occurred to me by intuition, and music is the
driving force behind this intuition."**

—Albert Einstein, physicist

One morning shortly after my husband, Andreas, and I were married, I
came into the main room of our mountain cabin in Lake Tahoe and found
him sitting still, tears in his eyes. A classical music piece from Chopin
filled the room with rich sound. He was completely immersed in the song.
I watched him, transfixed. As a child in Germany, he would gather with
his siblings and his parents in the evenings and listen to classical music—to
the patterns, instruments, structure, and dynamics. Unknown to the boy
who would at that time have preferred to be playing outside, his brain was
creating neural networks to hear, savor, and appreciate music.

When you listen to music mindfully, you're training your attention
and awareness, and you're becoming fully present to beauty and wonder.
Is music a regular part of your day already? Whether you plug into headphones on the train to work or you turn on your home speakers in the
evenings, focusing on a song provides another way of embedding another

mindfulness practice in your routine. Start by noticing the depth and structure, message and mood, and the melody and layers of harmonies within your chosen track, whether it's classical, blues, or rock-and-roll. As the music unfolds, try to identify themes, and then variations of those themes. Mozart's *12 Variations on "Twinkle, Twinkle, Little Star"* is a great composition for that particular exercise.

The mindfulness skills of concentration and open awareness can also heighten your direct experience with music. Ask yourself three things after you hit play:

> *What am I hearing?*
> *What am I sensing?*
> *What emotions, feelings, or thoughts are present for me?*

If you get distracted, gently return your focus to the music, just as you do with meditative breathing.

Today's highly cognitive society trains us to spend most of our time "in our heads"—thinking, analyzing, and planning. But music offers more than input for the brain. You can experience sound in an embodied way, as a "felt sense" that is more comprehensive and powerful than just listening with your ears or watching the movements of the players and instruments. Take a moment to recall the last time you were at a symphony, concert, show, or any other music event. Do you remember the sensations in your body as you were taking in the tunes?

In addition to listening with heightened awareness, you can practice the mindful quality of Beginner's Mind by letting go—of opinions, biases, and assumptions about genres, composers, and artists—and just be with the sounds. When you suspend judgment, you create an opening for wonder. This happened when I went to a Twenty One Pilots concert with my daughter, a performance I normally wouldn't have attended. I was surprised when I discovered how much I appreciated the depth of sound and rich variety that just two musicians could create.

When you immerse yourself in sound, listening can be a transformative experience. In a 2013 article, Mona Lisa Chanda and Daniel Levitin of McGill University observed that "music initiates brain stem responses that, in turn, regulate heart rate, pulse, blood pressure, body temperature, skin conductance, and muscle tension . . . " Music can also call forth a wide range of emotions and moods for us, turning wild elation into contentment, fear into peacefulness, sadness into joy. Or music can be used to generate excitement, energy, and more. Athletes use it to increase motivation; surgeons use it to deepen concentration; and office workers use it to enhance focus. Whatever your purpose, tapping into your playlist can be an intentional (and enjoyable) mindful break that integrates mind and body in a powerful way.

How:

1. **Select a new piece of music.** Experiment with listening to music you've never heard. You may have something novel in your own collection, or you might choose to turn the radio dial until something surprising catches your ear.

2. **Reduce distraction.** Close your eyes and put on headphones if you have them, or go into a quiet room. This will deepen your attention to what you're hearing.

3. **Adopt your Beginner's Mind.** Try not to judge the music by its genre, title, or artist's name before it has begun playing. Instead, ignore any labels and let yourself get lost in the journey of sound for the duration of the song.

4. **Practice nonjudgment.** Even if the music isn't your usual taste, let go of your mind's tendency to like or dislike it; maybe even try listening to what you normally dislike. Mindfulness is practicing nonjudgmental awareness. Allow yourself to explore the music fully, from composition to the sensations that it creates.

5. **Create music playlists for different moods.** A number of music services, such as Spotify, Pandora, and Apple Music, make it easy to create playlists to suit your mood or to even change a mindset. Take 15 minutes to sit, take a few deep breaths, and open up to the music you curated.

6. **Play an instrument.** Listen to music you make yourself, or in unison with others. Like taking photographs, playing an instrument syncs the attention of the mind with the body, and tunes the ear and heart to hear in the present moment.

7. **Recognize how music affects your emotions.** Music can connect you to feelings of joy and happiness (or to awe and tears, in my husband's case)—especially if it's music that you know and love. It can also happen with beautiful, strong, exquisite pieces of music that you're hearing for the first time. Relax and let whatever emotions occur to fully rise. Recognize them, name them, let them be.

29

Go for a walk

The practice of walking meditation is mindfulness in motion

• •

"The moment one gives close attention to anything, even a blade of grass, it becomes a mysterious, awesome, indescribably magnificent world in itself."

—Henry Miller, author

My favorite moments of my daughter's childhood are when she learned to walk—both times. Her first steps, on the very day she turned one, occurred in a burst across the wooden floor toward my mother's out-stretched arms. She started slowly, built momentum, and then flew forward, laughing with delight. The second time she learned to walk was at the age of seven, when the Buddhist monk Thich Nhat Hanh gently took her hand in his and they walked slowly, gently, and peacefully through a sun-filled green meadow at the Magnolia Grove Monastery in Mississippi. Ava Grace in her pale blue T-shirt, Thich Nhat Hanh in his brown robes. One step at a time, breathing in and breathing out naturally, in a walking meditation.

Walking meditation, or mindful walking, is a joyful way to practice mindfulness with movement, and an antidote to the frenetic pace that so many of us are used to these days. And it's perhaps one of the simplest ways to play. Mindful walking is as easy as lifting your foot, breathing in, putting your foot down heel first, then toes, and finally breathing out. It is about arriving, again and again, in each moment, by bringing your attention to your breath and to your foot touching the ground. As with sitting meditation, your mind will wander, and you will become distracted—but you can always return your attention to each foot making contact. Thich Nhat Hanh calls it "kissing the earth."

During mindful walking, you discover the stable feeling of the ground that is always there supporting you. If you're a person who always wants to do things "right," you can relax: There is no single right way to do this form of moving meditation. You can walk at a very slow pace, concentrating on each movement of each foot and coordinating your breath. You can also walk at a regular pace, or even move with speed. You can walk a mountain path or stake out a stretch of ground. As with every mindfulness practice in this book, I encourage you to experiment in the laboratory of your own life, and find ways to practice that fit your style, schedule, and location—indoors at home or work, or outside on a sidewalk or in nature.

Mindful walking is a core part of the corporate mindfulness programs I teach because so many find it to be an especially practical, accessible way to train concentration. It allows fidgety people who are so used to *doing* to practice focusing their attention and to move at the same time. During a recent program at Google in Zurich, Switzerland, the group of employees went outside and walked at a fairly slow pace on a gravel, tree-lined path near the Limmat River. It was a sight I won't forget—80 people moving slowly, intentionally, and with care for 15 minutes. Some walked back and forth in a line, others made a wide circle in the grass nearby, and others paced in one direction along the river. In this vibrant European city, passersby stopped and stared, trying to figure out what this unusual group exercise was all about.

A lively discussion always follows the mindful walking practice. One engineer told me that although he really struggles with sitting and meditating because he is so programmed to be in action all the time, he has found that mindful walking helps him quiet his mind and body through movement. A marketing manager described how she started out walking with a noisy mind, full of the usual work worries, as well as nervousness about what observers were thinking. After a few moments of practice, she realized that her racing mind had slowly started to settle, then she sensed her feelings of anxiety lessen. After a few more minutes she had a feeling of contentment and peace. From here, she could tune in to the world around her. She started to notice the beauty of the dark tree branches against the winter sky and the sound of the water moving in the river. During a Search Inside Yourself mindfulness program in Paris, a man came in on the second morning and told me, "I have lived in the same neighborhood for 20 years, and I never appreciated how beautiful it is until yesterday during my 15-minute mindful walk at dusk." If you stay attentive, a familiar path can be freshly illuminated. "New" experiences are another unsung benefit of mindfulness.

Mindful walking is another form of awareness and attention training—and as my coaching client Jon describes it, a practice of renewing the mind and body during the workday. Going on mindful walks is also a brilliant way to engage with kids. Children love it anytime adults are truly present and paying attention, sharing in their natural curiosity, wonder, and delight. That's why I treasure our evening family walks. My daughter likes to choose one of the senses, such as smell; we then stroll the street, bringing awareness to everything that hits our noses. You may recall from the entry on showering with awareness that the senses bring us right to the present, and you can apply that same principle on your mindful walks. Noticing smells, sights, and sounds trains your capacity to tune in to whatever is around you, effectively pulling you out of your head if you're ruminating, daydreaming, or thinking about anything other than what's happening in the moment.

Try to observe without getting lost in thought about what you're observing. There's a difference between noticing something and thinking about it. Can you simply see what is right there without your mind pivoting toward a stream of thoughts about what you are seeing (for example, seeing the apple tree without trying to recall all the ingredients in that apple pie recipe you love)? The same goes for your ability to *directly experience* the walk—can you feel the warm summer evening breeze on your face, the smell of honeysuckle as you walk by a blooming hedge, and if a memory of childhood is triggered, can you notice that you are becoming lost in thought and come right back to the scent or the breeze?

Another way to help you stay engaged in your direct experience is to look for ways that the season affects what you discover. In the spring, we find that the smell of our neighbors' yards is sweet and floral; in the summer, we savor a honeysuckle aroma; and in autumn, we relish the magnificent scent of fallen leaves. Your mindfulness skills of attention and awareness, along with all five senses, are fully alive during a mindful walk. There's a richness to life when we take in what's in front of us instead of rushing from A to B. You are exactly where you should be: right here, in the moment.

How: •

1. **Find a peaceful place to walk.** It can be in a park, along your neighborhood sidewalk, in the hallway at work, or in your living room. You can just walk in one direction, say from the office to the gym, or pick a place about 15 feet long and walk back and forth, slowly and mindfully. Enjoy letting go of the natural tendency to hurry to get somewhere.

2. **Begin by feeling your feet.** Start with standing meditation. Notice the sensation of making contact with the floor or ground. Feel your center, the core of your body. Breathe deeply, in and out of your center.

3. **Try slow, mindful walking.** Lift your right foot with awareness as you inhale. Put it down, heel first, then toes down as you exhale. Shift your weight to the right foot. Now attend to the other side. Lift your left foot with awareness, breathing in. Put it down, heel first, then place toes down, breathing out. Shift your weight to the right foot. Repeat, walking slowly for at least 10 minutes. When time permits, take longer mindful walks.

4. **Try mindful walking at a regular pace, using your senses.** Walk outdoors with a steady, easy, relaxed pace. You can practice open awareness as

you walk: Take in what is around you—sights, sounds, temperature, wind. Use your senses. Observe with an open, curious mind, without making up a story or explanation for whatever you notice.

5. **Witness your mind as you walk.** Notice where your attention goes. It's natural for your mind to wander or get distracted while walking. Bring yourself back to walking with focus and open awareness.

6. **Allow joy to arise.** Try it and you'll see: The practice of mindful walking, alone or with others, is an easy mindfulness activity that naturally cultivates a positive mood.

30

Create something

Experience the joy of focus and engagement by being a maker

• •

"If you hear a voice within you say, 'You cannot paint,' then by all means paint, and that voice will be silenced."

—Vincent Van Gogh, artist

We met once a month on a Saturday on the second floor of a red brick warehouse in northern Germany. Ten amateur painters and one professional artist who taught us, encouraged us, and pushed us when we were stuck. The group had been together for 30 years when I joined. We set up our easels in what became our usual spots, our backs toward the center of the room, our tubes of paint on side tables. On those days in the studio, from 10 a.m. to 5 p.m., I dropped into sustained focus and deep engagement. Much of the time, I was in a flow state, where I lost sense of time and place, immersed in the way the paint mixed on the palette, how it spread on the canvas, and how the lines and forms emerged.

Mihaly Csikszentmihaly, author of *Flow: The Psychology of Optimal Experience,* defines engagement as the extent to which you are immersed in the experience itself. Csikszentmihaly says flow occurs when full engagement creates a sustainable feeling of energized involvement and enjoyment, just as I experienced in my Saturday painting sessions.

Anything that is challenging and requires focus, skill, and mastery, as most creative pursuits do, is practice for mindful attention. Whether it's composing a musical piece, decorating, painting, or writing, your leisure activities can lead you to a flow state.

In a 2016 interview, Krista Tippett spoke with Elizabeth Gilbert, the author of *Eat, Pray, Love* and *Big Magic: Creative Living Beyond Fear,* about the joy of creativity and deep engagement. "Being creative is achieving a state of sublime focus," Gilbert observed. She calls creativity "magic" and suggests that it is part of our "shared human inheritance," like DNA. Sometimes it's easy to forget that we are all descendants of makers: Our ancestors worked with their hands and crafted everything they needed. For them, it was necessary for survival—but it might be equally essential to us as an ingredient for flourishing.

Remember that creating does not necessarily mean making something elaborate—nor does your final product have to last forever. Making art that is impermanent can just as easily inspire an emotional response: wonder that exists only in the moment. In a 2010 article, filmmaker and artist Helen Plumb, inspired by Descartes, observed that "[t]he emotion of wonder is a passion of the soul . . . It produces a feeling of surprise that is present with something that is rare and extraordinary." Letting go of your handiwork can enhance this sense.

When I was in India on a trip to teach mindfulness at Google Hyderabad, I stayed at a healing Ayurvedic retreat before heading to the city. One afternoon, my Sikh friend Ben and I painted a mandala on the rich, dark hardwood floor of the entranceway using bright pink, blue, green, and yellow sands. When Buddhist monks create mandalas, millions of colorful sand grains are painstakingly laid into place on a flat platform over a period of several days, forming an intricate diagram of the enlightened mind and the ideal world. The art lasts for only a few days before being wiped away. As we worked on our smaller, one-afternoon version, knowing that the beauty was temporary and would be gone tomorrow only heightened my attention and wonder. And as the monks had taught, I found the exercise in itself to be a joyful meditation, symbolizing life's transitionary stages of creation and destruction.

You don't need to go to India to explore your creativity, though; you can find ways to tap into your inner artist daily. You could take a watercolor kit, paper, and a jar of water to a local park and experiment with color, just allowing whatever happens to emerge when the brush meets the paper. Or, you might plate some beautiful food; get dressed with attention to line, color, and proportion; or arrange a dinner table with layers of color, texture, and flickering light. Talent and other people's value of the work don't matter here; this is purely about doing and *your* experience.

Consider the best conditions for you to create. It might require that you carve out time alone. Lin-Manuel Miranda, the writer, producer, and star of the epic Broadway musical *Hamilton,* has said, "Time alone is the gift of self-entertainment—and that is the font of creativity." How can you find ways to block time for artistic endeavors, and set the scene to deepen your engagement and enjoyment? Ideally, I like to have music playing (without words), natural light, and, if the weather is right, open windows. See what works for you, and arrange your space and schedule to accommodate it.

How: ···································

1. **Seek out regular creative play.** Whether you join a painting group, a pottery studio, or a furniture-building class, find an activity that suits your interests and sign up. If committing to a class sounds like too much, start with a single drop-in session or workshop.

2. **Immerse yourself in a creative project.** Do you have a chair that you have wanted to restore? A photo album to make? The desire to paint the living room gray? Choose a project, set a deadline, and bring mindful attention and your nonjudging mind to it.

3. **Designate daily time to create something.** Like the Buddhist monks devoting time to their sand mandalas, make time in your normal day to consciously create something, even if it is simply how you arrange the food on your plate at lunchtime. Creativity can be embroidered into your everyday life.

4. **Find your optimal conditions for creativity.** What environment works best for you? Is it better to leave out the art materials so you can drop right in, as my artist brother Johnny always advised? Do you need a peaceful spot in your home? Are you more supported in a group?

5. **Host an art party.** Invite friends for a "create something" party. Set out paint, large and small canvases, collage materials, oil pastels, chalks, or other material on different tables. With good food and music, spend the evening dabbling, creating, exploring, and having fun. Or, if you enjoy the social experience but aren't ready to host, find a "wine and design" class to attend or something similar in your area.

31

Engage with your children

Be truly present at your kids' activities

• •

"Tell me to what you pay attention and I will tell you who you are."
—José Ortega y Gasset, Spanish philosopher

My daughter plays soccer on a team made up of some of my favorite people—and I'm not talking about the kids. I mean the parents. The soccer team has played together for 11 seasons, and the parents are now a band of friends in their own right. We lead busy lives and it's fun to reunite on Saturdays at the games. But we often miss the magical moments on the field, because we're caught up in catching up.

One cost of missing such moments is the sheer joy we adults could be getting in savoring them. But the cost to our children from our lack of engagement can be even greater. Over the years, myriad studies and articles have evaluated quality versus quantity time in parenting, with quantity generally losing out. A groundbreaking study from the University of Toronto, published in 2015, found that the quantity of time that parents, and moms in particular, spend with their kids from ages three through adolescence has virtually no relationship to how they turn out—not in math and reading scores, not in emotional well-being, and not in behavior. The exception, the researchers discovered, is that spending more time with teenagers in busy and hectic urban environments can keep them out of trouble. And it is interesting to note that the researchers found that time spent with sleep-deprived and stressed-out parents can even be harmful. Yet, with all the research, few studies have addressed the subtler idea of how truly *engaging* with your children during the time you spend with them can positively affect you both. This is where mindfulness can be a game changer.

The good news is that if you have kids in your life (yours or someone else's), schedules these days are full of activities—a Little League game or swim meet, a ballet performance or school play—that are ripe for mindful adult-child engagement. When you are truly present, you remember what's most important, and the value of being there for it. You are there to witness the skillful goal, the exquisite pirouette, the surprising choral solo.

On the surface, this idea of engagement—of truly focusing on your child—may seem simple. But in reality, there are internal and external distractions to navigate. When you get sidetracked, which can happen in any mindfulness activity, the task is to gently notice and bring your attention back to the child you treasure. But, as we've learned, being mindful is about more than paying attention. In an oft-cited mindfulness paper from 2005, social psychology researcher and author Shauna Shapiro framed mindfulness as having three elements: intention, attention, and attitude. In addition to being attentive to your child on the field, for example, you can also use mindful awareness to notice your own attitude. Try observing *how* you are relating to your child during his or her performance. Do you have a mindset of open, nonjudgmental awareness, and ultimately compassion?

As always, you can get clues to your mindset by tuning in to your body's signals. Do you notice clenched fists? An anxious or excited heartbeat? What emotions underlie these sensations? Could you be overidentifying with your child's ability? If the child is doing well, what thoughts are you having? If the child is watching birds fly overhead and missing key plays, what's happening in your mind?

Mindfulness can help you let go of judging your child and yourself, and help you cultivate acceptance and compassion instead. Remember that curious self-inquiry is a counter-mindset to judgment. When you notice that you're having thoughts like, *She is just not coordinated* or *He is not making an effort* or *I dropped the ball as a parent—I don't support him enough in practicing,* take a mindful pause. Go through the four questions that author Byron Katie made famous in her method of self-inquiry, called The Work:

1. What am I believing? (About my child? About myself as a parent?)
2. How do I know this is true?
3. How would I feel without this thought?
4. What is the antidote to this thought—the opposite statement?

This practice can help you strengthen your inner observer, and help you recognize when your judging mind might be creating distance, instead of connection, with your child. Watch out for "comparing mind" too; comparing a child to siblings or others also detracts from simply being present and engaged with your children just as they are, right now.

The same mindfulness precepts carry into play with your kids. Children of all ages will readily pick up the energy and quality of your attention. They know if you're engaged or not. Are you distracted when reading a book to them? Are you tuned out while at the playground because you're constantly checking your text and email? Even the presence of a mobile phone on a dinner table reduces engagement.

The question to keep asking yourself is how emotionally connected and present you are when you're with your kids. This approach goes beyond quantity and quality evaluations—and with mindfulness, the answer and the solution will become clear.

How: ....

1. **Plan engaging activities.** Look at your weekly schedule and see where you can spend time with a child that involves being together in an emotionally connected way—such as building a Lego kit, creating some art, or gardening—rather than sitting side-by-side watching a TV screen.

2. **Decide where to direct attention.** Try to sustain your attention with a clear intention, the heart of mindfulness. It takes practice, so be patient if you find yourself watching the game and then jumping in to a conversation with another parent yet again. When you realize it, just bring your focus back to your child.

3. **Practice underreacting.** Whether you're watching your kid from the sidelines or facing off with her directly in a board game, work on pausing before reacting. When you feel yourself get emotionally triggered, note it: *Oh, here it is—I'm getting triggered by my view of fairness, or my idea of how my kid should be playing.* Recognize the thought, create space for taking a few breaths, and then remind yourself of your intention for being there. With practice, you are strengthening the quality of equanimity.

4. **Let go of your agenda.** You think your young athlete will get more action and glory playing offense, but your kid prefers to play defense. With observation, you can see your motivations, your hidden agenda. Not all of your goals are necessarily harmful, but try to be aware of when your resistance is getting in the way of the engagement, play, and joy that's available to you and your child when you let go.

5. **Connect to wonder.** Where attention goes, energy flows. Train your mind to notice the good, positive moments, the new skills. Did you notice the caring, helping actions of your kid as he or she interacted with others? What skills seem to be getting stronger? Can you observe and comment on the effort your child is harnessing when rehearsing a play, practicing ballet, or attempting a lacrosse goal? Share your delight in witnessing a young person developing, growing, and having fun.

32

Get outside

Unplug and immerse yourself in nature
to rejuvenate and access wonder

. . . .

"Nature's peace will flow into you as sunshine flows into trees."

—John Muir, naturalist, author

The storm blew into our Maryland neighborhood quite unexpectedly one warm Saturday in November a few years ago. The day had been calm; people were riding bikes in T-shirts in what would normally be a chilly season. Suddenly, the tall old trees in our yard began to sway wildly in the strong wind. Bright yellow, orange, and red leaves rained down, swirling in all directions. My daughter, Ava Grace, and I ran to the middle of the yard, arms outstretched, heads tilted back, faces to the sky, dashing left and right. We were catching leaves and couldn't help shouting out our discoveries—"The oak leaves fall more slowly! . . . The maple 'propellers' can fly horizontally . . . The bright yellow elm leaves come down all at once!" After an hour of running and yelling, we collapsed on the grass, feeling joyful, relaxed, and connected to each other.

According to research, these powerful effects of being outside are not unusual. Scientists around the world are demonstrating what philosophers, artists, and poets such as John Muir, Ansel Adams, Henry David

Thoreau, and Mary Oliver have long known: Being in nature has a significant impact on your brain, physiology, and well-being. In a 2015 *National Geographic* magazine article, cognitive psychologist and avid backpacker David Strayer describes measuring the brain waves of subjects who had spent time in nature. He found that when people are outside, the brain's prefrontal cortex—the part of your brain engaged in attentional control, planning, and decision-making—can take a needed break. Taking care of your brain is akin to working out with weights: You have periods of muscle contraction with use, and periods of rest, both of which are essential. After examining heart rate, protein markers, stress hormones, and other physiological factors, Strayer concluded that when we spend time in nature, "something profound is going on."

In a 2014 study done in Finland, researchers found evidence of the impact of nature on how rejuvenated and restored subjects felt. Seventy-seven participants visited three different types of urban areas: a built-up city center, an urban park, and an urban woodland located in Helsinki. They found that even short-term visits to natural areas can have positive effects on perceived stress relief compared to visiting a developed, man-made environment. The urban park and urban woodland had almost the same positive outcomes on vitality, mood, and creativity, but the overall winner in perceived levels of rejuvenation was being out in the woods. So if you're a city dweller, hit your local park; if you're in the countryside, get out into wild. And if you enjoy running, can you move your workout from the treadmill to the park to optimize your well-being benefits?

A team in Japan found that being in the woods for as little as 15 minutes can cause measurable positive changes in physiology. In the experiment, the researchers sent 84 participants out walking in seven different forests, while the same number of volunteers walked around city centers. The payoff for the nature walkers was strong: They showed a decrease in the stress hormone cortisol, a drop in blood pressure, and a reduced heart rate.

From exploring the woods with my four brothers and sister as a child, to hiking the Kalalau Trail on the Napali coast of Kauai, I have always loved the way being in nature makes me feel both joyful and at peace. Over the years, I've heard about the profound effects of nature directly from many attendees of my mindfulness talks. One, a journalist from Washington, D.C., described how being in nature affects her in an almost primal way, as if her body responds physically to the trees, air, and earth, and begins to shift to a peaceful state. A corporate executive told me, "When I'm outside in the wilderness, I feel connected as if on a unified stage. When I'm in nature I feel part of one, universal thing. The result for me is joy."

Lisa Nisbet, a psychology professor from Trent University in Canada, agrees that being in nature nourishes us. She suggests that "people under-estimate the happiness effect" of being outdoors. "We don't think of it as a way to increase happiness. We think other things will, like shopping or TV." What we do in our unscheduled time is often habitual. Try to notice that moment before you decide to pick up the remote or head to the mall, and create space by taking a few breaths. Then choose to head out into nature instead—to a local park, garden, or walking trail. Mindfulness allows you to become a witness to your leisure time patterns, and consider whether or not your go-to activities actually make you happy. If you automatically cruise the Internet in your free hours, notice if you feel refreshed and joyful after. If not, make a deliberate choice to get fresh air.

You can create your own natural retreat by bringing mindfulness outdoors. Walking along a freshwater creek and listening to the current move over rocks can settle your mind and body. So can standing at the edge of the ocean, watching the surf slide over the sand. In these moments in nature, you can send good wishes out to the world with a mini-practice of loving-kindness. My teaching partner Lori kayaks in the sparkling solitude of a river, breathing mindfully in sync with her paddle dipping into the water. Brothers Pax and Roan hike for hours under an expansive sky above California's Muir Beach to quiet the mind, and then they sit on the ground, connecting to the earth, and tuning in with all the senses to what is all around them. By spending more time in the open air, you will discover what makes you feel alive, grounded, and peaceful.

Nature unifies our senses, minds, and bodies. It can be breathtaking to tune in to the interconnection of all things in the natural world. I'm constantly drawn to the sense of wonder that emerges when I'm outdoors:

the sense that I am just one small element in a vast, miraculous ecosystem, shimmering and vibrating with life. Even on the most hectic days, the act of stepping outside allows your nervous system to calm, your cognitive centers to rest, and your mood to lift. It is a no-cost therapy with no side effects. It gives you interior space to focus on the goodness and joy available to you in each moment of your life.

How:

1. **Time travel to find outdoor play activities.** Close your eyes and think back to your childhood. What were the things you loved to do in nature in your free time? Making dams in the creek after the rain? Pancakes out of clay? I loved swimming in cool freshwater lakes. Remember your favorites, and try them now—alone or with others.

2. **Lose the headphones when you play outside.** It's wonderful to be outside under the sun or stars, but do so in a way that allows you to tune in to the sounds of the environment instead of your favorite podcast.

3. **Look at a tree.** Be where you are. When you are swimming, hiking, playing catch in nature, try to be there. Notice where your mind is and bring it back to the present activity, savoring the experience. Looking at a tree is a simple and immediate way to anchor yourself in the here and now. That is the only place the tree ever is.

4. **Play in nature at the edge of your comfort zone.** Hike a trail that might be higher than your usual walks, kayak white water, spend an afternoon at a high-ropes adventure park in tall trees, swim across a wide lake (with a companion, of course). Outdoor activities that stretch your abilities require concentration. Experiencing flow is highly likely in these moments when you are engaged with your mind and body in sync. This is where joy emerges.

5. **Bring your meditation practice outdoors.** Why not bring your favorite practices, whether mindful breathing, a body scan, loving-kindness, or taking in the good, to your next outdoor excursion? Notice the effect of combining nature with the nourishing mindfulness practices that you have been enjoying at home and in the office.

33

Visit a museum

Soaking up good art can be an act of mindful presence, wonder, and awe

· ·

"Find joy in the sky, in the trees, in the flowers. There are always flowers everywhere for those who want to see them."

—Henri Matisse, artist

A friend emailed me recently to ask for advice: She said she cannot seem to get away from emotional rants and disturbing announcements in the news, on Facebook, and on other social media. She was looking for ideas to help her relax and enjoy the breaks in her days. I suggested she hop on the D.C. Metro and visit a museum.

Museums call forth the part of you that wants to see, connect, and attend. In a museum you move slowly, breathe deeply, and tune in to your surroundings. It's easy to let go of worries; forget about politics, work, and family matters; and find peace among masterpieces of human endeavor. Being in a museum directs focus away from yourself and gives wider perspective. You can often see works that are centuries old; it is a cultural experience of interconnection with fellow humans across geography, space, and time.

Susan Pollak, a co-founder of the Center for Mindfulness and Compassion at Harvard Medical School, and Dr. Elizabeth Gaufberg, associate professor of psychiatry, guide new medical residents through museums to help them relieve stress and retain their empathy through a difficult and intense year of treating patients. According to Gaufberg, when you visit a museum, "There's something that happens where you're really in the moment noticing. You're not ruminating on something that happened yesterday, and that's incredibly stress relieving." That's because being in the present, focusing attention on a painting, sculpture, or a photograph, *is* a moment of mindfulness. "Being in front of a work of art helps us get there," says Pollak. "It's a refuge from the craziness of our lives."

You can go to a museum spontaneously or visit one regularly as part of your mindfulness practice. Julia Cameron, an active artist for more than three decades, calls this an "artist date" and describes it as "assigned play" in her landmark book *The Artist's Way*. Meant to jolt you out of the boredom, inertia, or autopilot that takes over when you get too busy, "assigned play" means making regular dates to choose something interesting, special, and out of your normal routine, and then doing it alone. Author Anne Lamott sees Cameron's idea of assigned play as a technique for paying attention—because, after all, that's what experiencing art is all about.

Visiting a museum can be a mindful experience beyond looking at the art it contains. Museum buildings have become examples of art in their own right. Some of the world's best architects have competed to win the prize of designing stunning museum spaces. You can step into the Getty in Los Angeles, the Guggenheim or Museum of Modern Art (MoMA) in New York City, the Broad at Michigan State University, or any number of international institutions of architectural beauty and have a mindful retreat just by looking at the structure itself.

Whether it's a world-renowned site or a local gem, visiting a museum gives you a 360-degree mindfulness experience. When you pause in front of a painting or under a hanging sculpture, or stand transfixed inside a darkened room to enjoy a visual media presentation, you get the joy of tuning in to creative expression and of being connected to works and themes greater than yourself.

How:

1. **"Go to art."** This is what my friend Robert says when I ask him what he and his wife, Amy, do on the weekends. Scan the newspaper or search online to find out what is being exhibited—or be spontaneous and just show up.

2. **Try mindful museum walking.** Ground yourself in the space by stopping and bringing focus to your feet. Take a few breaths to disengage your autopilot and wake up your sense of alertness. Begin walking slowly, using open awareness to know you are moving among artworks and people, and also to bring attention to your body.

3. **Find a piece of art that calls to you.** Notice the artist, the time period, the artistic style. Be aware of the context in which the piece was made, and of the miracle that you are able to stand in front of it right now.

4. **See with a wide-angle and a zoom lens.** Begin mindful looking with a few breaths. Tune in to your direct experience of the art without getting lost in thought. Start with a broader view and take in the whole composition: the mood, palette, textures, light. Use your Beginner's Mind. Then bring your focus to one detail in the work: a puffy cloud in the blue sky of a Canaletto landscape, a tiny triangle in a Matisse cutout, a dangling piece of a Calder mobile.

5. **Receive sense impressions in the body.** Experience art with your whole body. Do a mini-body scan to tune in to any sensations in your body and the emotions that go with them. Are any emotions arising? Notice them, allow them, see them as a witnessing observer to your experience.

6. **Sketch, draw, color, or paint.** If you're inclined, have fun sketching something after you see the art. With curiosity, lightness, and wonder, see what comes out on the paper with whatever creative tools you brought along. Don't judge; just let go and enjoy!

34

Travel with curiosity and wonder

Cultivate an inner witness that is present, open, and inquisitive

. . . .

"My destination is no longer a place, rather a new way of seeing."

—Marcel Proust, author

As I slept in the next hotel room, my teaching partner Hemant sprang out of bed in Helsinki at 5:00 a.m. and jumped into a taxi to catch a flight to London. He wanted to give himself plenty of time because the flight was important—he was going to meet his elderly father before joining me again to teach in Munich. Hemant sat patiently in the waiting area and then did a double take when he read the announcement board again, realizing with a jolt that he was in the wrong terminal. He had misread the information about the gate and was about to board a codeshare flight to the same city, but his ticket was not for that airplane. His heart pounded, cortisol and adrenaline pumped through his body, and his mind raced with problem-solving ideas. Being a mindfulness teacher, he actually observed this physical reaction as if he were watching a slow-motion movie. He texted me later: "It was interesting watching it happen!"

When you travel, you will inevitably experience a journey of ups and downs. Although you plan, reserve, and confirm your trip, you can experience flight delays, missed trains, a favorite coat left in the overhead bin or a wallet in a taxi—even an unexpected illness. But if you activate the mindset of acceptance over resistance and access compassion instead of judgment, you can observe your body's responses and witness the power of your physiology when it mobilizes you into action instead of feeling stressed and upset.

When Hemant realized what happened, he could have easily let his inner critic berate him: "How could I have misread the flight number? Oh no, the flight-change fees!" Instead, even though he felt his body activate the stress response, he was able to act skillfully. He harnessed the flood of adrenaline to bolt through the airport. Mindfulness doesn't mean stopping and sitting with your eyes closed in the middle of a challenging travel moment; it means having the ability to see clearly without judgment—it gives you the ability to take skillful action. Hemant made it to London and reunited with his dad.

Mindfulness helps you meet the unexpected challenges of travel with equanimity, but there's another significant benefit: the way you experience your entire trip. There's beauty present in any moment if you're able to be there for it with the freshness of a curious child, and a foreign place can be great for practicing this. You can see the way waiters move like synchronized swimmers, the glow of city lights at dusk, the golden autumn sun that cuts across your path on an afternoon hike. Being mindful, which is not something we habitually do, is necessary to notice beauty. Usually we obscure it with our endless evaluations (*The service is slow here*), comparisons (*In my city you get water without asking*), categorizations (*Just another temple, church altar, or city square*), or needs (*I would love an iced tea and they don't have it, bummer*). When you can suspend these internal voices that are driven by mental habits, the incredible uniqueness of the experience opens up to you. If you catch yourself in these patterns, activate curiosity instead: *I wonder what the favorite beverage is here? What influenced the design of this altar? What is daily life like here?*

You'll find mindfulness inherently supportive of being "in the now," a phrase that spiritual teacher and author Eckhart Tolle uses often. When you're exploring the narrow side streets of a city you've never been to before, smelling the grass in a countryside that's unfamiliar, or tasting the flavors of food that you're eating for the first time, you want to be right there, connecting to the wonder of it. Use your breath to anchor your attention in these moments. There is no place on your trip where you cannot pause and notice your breath, and tune in to the beauty and joy available.

Travel hurls you into the unknown; it's unpredictable and invigorating. But sometimes you long for the familiar. Try to create mindful routines in a new location where you'll be staying for any length of time. In Copenhagen, I found a small, cozy café near my hotel that I went to every day for breakfast and journaling. In Paris, I found a beautiful park near my Airbnb that I dropped into after teaching to ground myself in the familiar. Wherever I am, I keep a morning mindfulness routine of mindful breathing, loving-kindness, and setting intentions, which keeps me centered and connected to a daily rhythm. I also travel with a silk pouch containing a candle, a photo of my family, and my mindfulness bell. The bell's clear sound is an integral part of my mindfulness practice and a peaceful way to harness my attention and bring me home to my inner sanctuary, wherever I am.

Travel also helps you become stronger at being with uncertainty and impermanence, which is how life really is anyway. Things are changing in a more noticeable way than in normal daily life. A rented apartment starts to feel like home and then you have to leave. New relationships can be intense and then you must say goodbye. When you realize you start clinging, or resisting the end of the experience, see if you can switch to take in the good to savor the happiness of what you have right now.

The key to mindful travel is not wishing things were different. Instead, practice being present. When you travel with open eyes, you can explore other places, cultures, and people and expand your horizons: not only a pleasurable experience, but also a self-confidence builder that adds a sense of connection to a greater whole. You start to see that no matter where you are, the humanity we share with others far outweighs the differences. Beauty is present in any moment that we allow to happen. I spend a big part of my life traveling, and mindfulness allows me to be fully alive with discovery, joy, and gratitude on every trip.

How: •

1. **Drop expectations.** In each step of your journey, just allow it to be whatever it is, without having expectations that set you up for the roller coaster of emotions tied to elation and disappointment. Go into new situations and new cultures and meet new people without expecting them to be a certain way. Learn the phrase, "So this is what this is like."

2. **Transform waiting into a mindfulness session.** When you find yourself waiting to check in, retrieve luggage, or get moving in stalled traffic, take a mindful pause. Feel your feet making contact with the ground. Take three, slow, relaxing breaths, noticing each exhale. Silently send loving-kindness wishes to those around you who are also waiting, as you realize you are all in this together.

3. **Let go of comparing the strange to the familiar.** Forget comparing the dark, thick coffee in Turkey to your favorite morning joe from the deli outside your office; just bring an open, curious Beginner's Mind to sipping the drink, as if you've never had it before.

4. **Use mindfulness practices to start your day and get to sleep.** Schedules and time zones can turn you upside down. Plan time to sit still and practice mindful breathing before you start your day. If you have jet lag, do a body scan or loving-kindness meditation until you get sleepy.

5. **Choose your focus.** You can focus on what's missing, challenging, or uncomfortable—or you can focus on what is good, caring, and beautiful. As the streetcar takes you to your hotel after a delayed flight and unhealthy airline food, are you lost in thought, ruminating and complaining? Or are you looking out of the window, noticing unique buildings, wild gardens, and smiling people on bikes as you drive by?

6. **Keep a travel journal.** Pack a small, lightweight notebook to keep with you. Pay closer attention to your emotions, observations, and insights as you travel by writing about them. Take breaks in the day, focus on the good, and record your feelings. Then read your journal often.

Love:
Enrich the Day

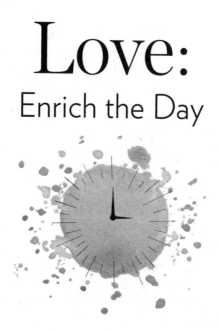

As we've moved through the dimensions of a mindful day—at home, work, and play—I've shared practices and integrated qualities that you can use to optimize your moment-to-moment experience. Now we come to love. Every single quality of mindfulness has everything to do with love; there is no mindfulness practice without love, and vice versa. Buddhist scholar Jack Kornfield says, "The point of mindfulness is not to perfect yourself; it is to perfect your love." It's more than a positive emotion: Love is a positive state that you can cultivate, and it permeates every aspect of life.

Mindfulness skills and attitudes can help you achieve this task by helping you look at yourself closely and allowing your heart to open. Habits of our mind often get in the way of experiencing love in a clear, embodied way. To love yourself and others requires that you cut through the expectations, assumptions, comparisons, worries, fears, or sense of unworthiness that block your ability to connect. It takes conscious effort to be willing to see and challenge the stories we tell ourselves—but it's worth it to take down the walls and free ourselves to embrace imperfections, forgive, and love fully. In the coming pages, I'll share concrete ways that you can strengthen your connection with your family, your friends, and most of all, yourself. Relationships are the connections in your life that have the potential to be "a sacred refuge, a place of healing and awakening" as mindfulness teacher and psychologist Tara Brach puts it. She emphasizes the idea of looking deeply at one's self and at one another: "With each person we meet, we can learn to look behind the mask and see the one who longs to love and be loved. Most of us need to be reminded that we are good, that we are lovable, that we belong." The skills and qualities of mindfulness can guide you toward seeing with fresh eyes and living with compassion and kindness.

Mindful training in love is never done. But you will notice it comes more easily as you open your heart in the practices that follow. When you're present with loving awareness, you can allow the joy that arises from loving to unfurl. It begins with learning to love yourself, and expands out from there, in ever-widening circles.

35

Welcome one another

Make the act of receiving another a moment of presence and love

● ●

"Whether or not we follow any particular spiritual tradition, the benefits of love and kindness are obvious to anyone."

—Tenzin Gyatso, the 14th Dalai Lama

Our golden retriever Beau was our master teacher in how to greet a loved one. There were days when he would almost knock my husband over after work, meeting him at the front door with happy crying, enthusiastic tail wagging, and a big smile. When Beau died, his evening greeting was noticeably absent. But a few days later, my daughter and I had an idea: When we heard the doorknob turn, we would run to the door, hugging and kissing my husband in a pretty good imitation of Beau. Our dog had taught us how to show love by sincerely welcoming the people we care about into our orbit.

We all yearn for connection—to be seen, appreciated, and loved. Yet in our society, many of us feel isolated and are touch-deprived. Moments of transition can be an easy way for you to connect and be more present for those you care about. In addition to the benefit of demonstrating to the person that "you matter, and I care," a mindful greeting with a hug can make you and the other person happier and healthier. A hug increases levels of the "love hormone" oxytocin, and reduces the harmful effects of stress, which can benefit your heart health and more. One study from the University of North Carolina found that women who hugged their spouse or partner frequently (even for just 20 seconds) had lower blood pressure. Often when we are welcoming someone—whether home from a long day, to a planned dinner, or even to an important meeting—that person is coming from crawling traffic, a difficult encounter, or another potentially stressful situation. A welcoming physical gesture conveys safety and trust. Neuroscientist Michele Noonan says a warm touch can create an instant attitude makeover and can ease a person's level of irritation because the sensation triggers the insula, a region in the brain involved with emotional processing. That's why some experts suggest that to build connection, we hold our hug until both bodies feel relaxed.

We received training on this at Thich Nhat Hanh's monastery at the Magnolia Grove Meditation Practice Center in Mississippi, when the nuns and monks taught us the hugging meditation as part of a family mindfulness ritual. Of course, the hugging meditation can be done anytime, not just as a greeting. The practice builds on the mindfulness qualities of awareness, generosity, and joy. First you bow and recognize the presence of each other—for example, walking to the door, making eye contact and saying "Welcome home," or standing and truly acknowledging that someone has arrived to join you for a meal. Then each of you take a conscious breath to bring yourself fully into the moment. Next, you open your arms and hug, holding each other for three in-and-out breaths.

With the first breath, you are aware that *you are present* in this very moment and that you are happy. With the second breath, you are aware that *the other* is present in this moment and that you are happy about this as well. With the third breath, you are aware that *both of you* are here *together,* right now, and you feel deep gratitude and joy for your togetherness. After the third breath, release the hug and bow to each other to express your thanks. As Thich Nhat Hanh teaches, this process makes the message clear: "Darling, you are precious to me."

Remember that presence is the ultimate loving gift you can give, and receive.

How:

1. **Stop when you hear a knock at the door.** Anytime you are about to encounter a loved one, pause, take a breath, and open the door or face the person. You are shifting your focus to welcoming him or her.

2. **Make eye contact, smile, and breathe.** When welcoming with attention and intention, don't act rushed or start downloading about your day. Connection starts with the eyes. Think about making the other person feel seen by looking him or her directly in the eye and turning your body to face him or her.

3. **Do a simple hugging meditation.** For family and close friends, teach this practice, or guide them through the three-breath practice of mindful connection. Facing one another, open your arms and hug. Take three breaths together, allowing the gratitude of being close to arise naturally. On the first breath, be grateful to be alive. On the second breath, be grateful that the other person is alive. On the third breath, be grateful that you are in this moment together.

4. **Sense and reflect.** Turn your attention inward, noticing how your body feels after a warm connection, whether it's a hug or another way of greeting. Savor that sensation; you are taking in the good with gratitude, and living more consciously.

36

Love yourself

Kind attention with compassion is at the heart of loving yourself

. . . .

"The more one does and sees and feels, the more one is able to do."

—Amelia Earhart, aviation pioneer, author

The first time I remember seeing the phrase "love yourself" was on the cover of an early issue of Oprah's *O* magazine. I heard it here and there after that, but I didn't *get* it. I loved myself in a distant, conceptual way, but I didn't know how to translate that into everyday living. Only later would I understand what it meant to love myself fully, in vivid detail, with wonder and joy. Self-love includes all aspects of who you are—the joy, the sorrow, the noblest acts, the moments of regret, the inner land-scape, the outer actions, the difficult past, the unknown future. And mindfulness skills give you the capacity to embrace all of it with kind awareness and compassion.

Loving yourself begins with the orientation of your mind. Ann Weiser Cornell, an expert in the mindfulness practice of focusing, describes the qualities of friendship that we can give to ourselves. These include allowing, patience, curiosity, respect, warmth, compassion, and love. It is especially powerful when you shift how you treat yourself during hard times. By paying attention to whatever was difficult, I started to allow my feelings to be there—to simply observe them as a "witness," without judgment, as we've been practicing throughout the book. In this case, it might sound something like this: *Oh, it's like this right now.* I use inquiry to investigate my thoughts, beliefs, and emotions, and to notice what's happening deeper below the surface. I ask myself: *What are you believing? What hurts? What do you need?* Loving myself means talking to myself as I would to a friend. Instead of listening to a critical, unsympathetic inner voice when I failed *(Why didn't you . . . ? You shouldn't have . . . You never . . . You are so . . .),* I learned a voice of compassion and kindness: *That's okay,* or *This is a hard time right now for you; accept it,* or *Yes, you dropped a ball; it's not unusual.* I've found that learning to be compassionate with myself during difficult times can be transformative. It is the kind of love a mother extends to a crying child: the unconditional, generous, all-encompassing feeling that allows a child to let go of pain and be open to love.

And I learned to love myself on the outside. At a health coaching session at my house, my friend Trina, a medical doctor, professor, and integrative health coach, asked me to face myself in a full-length mirror. I visibly winced. As was my habit, my attention went to what I didn't like: new wrinkles, more cushion in the waist, the sun freckles from a bad sunburn when I was 18. Trina then asked me to point out what I loved about the reflection I saw. I stood a while before answering. I opened my heart, and my eyes. "I love the color of my eyes. I love my collarbones. I love my legs." In that tender moment, I saw a beautiful woman standing there: one who had loved deeply, overcome illness, competed in a triathlon, and given birth without drugs. It was a deep shift for me: I let go of wishing anything was different. Trina encouraged me to see myself this way each time I looked in the mirror, and to say, "Laurie, I love you." It might sound strange to imagine saying that to yourself—but it is possible to accept yourself in the way that parents do their children: completely.

When you start to cultivate deeper loving awareness, you become more conscious of the ways you care for yourself, or not. While I was growing my company, parenting a school-age child, and managing an international teaching schedule, I didn't see a doctor for almost two years. Self-care fell to the bottom of a full list. But with my new intention to love myself more, I used my rational, planning brain to initiate helpful behaviors. I saw my doctor more regularly, and increased my yoga and hiking routines. I started wearing lovely French lingerie that celebrated my feminine side.

Self-love goes even deeper with heart-centered practice. Since the time I could walk, my mother taught me to pray for others, which meant taking time each evening to bless friends, family, and loved ones. As an adult, I learned to bless myself also, using the practice of loving-kindness. I do so in my morning routine, after mindful breathing, by repeating phrases carrying good wishes directed first to me and then expanding out to others:

> *May I be happy,*
> *May I be healthy.*
> *May I live with grace and ease.*
> *May I know that I am loved.*

Create your own blessing or set of phrases and practice them. What you practice grows stronger. Over time, the phrase "love yourself" will become less distant and conceptual, and you will experience a more direct, action-oriented relationship with yourself.

Actress Lucille Ball knew this well: "Love yourself first and everything else falls into line." We hear the same message when we're strapped into our seat belts on an airplane, preparing for takeoff. In the airplane and in life, put the oxygen mask on yourself first. Then you will be able to take care of—and love—those around you.

How:

1. **Start the day by wishing yourself well.** Prime your mind and heart to love yourself. Send yourself good wishes in the morning with a self-directed loving-kindness meditation. If it feels strange to send blessings to yourself, bring to mind those who love you dearly and imagine that they are sending the wishes.

2. **Set the intention to treat yourself with love.** It all begins with intention to water the seeds of choice for positive growth: Go with love, rather than sabotaging, hurting, punishing, or overindulging yourself.

3. **Pay attention to how you talk to yourself.** When you notice that you are judging, blaming, or scolding, you are not in a state of loving presence. Stop. Take a breath. Let go of resisting the situation and talk to yourself as you would a good friend. Ask yourself, *What is the most loving thing I can do for myself right now?*

4. **Practice the three gestures of love.** These combine a physical gesture (such as putting your hand on your heart or placing your palms together when being grateful) to anchor your body with phrases of kindness, love, and gratitude. You might say, *It's okay* to soothe yourself with kindness; *I love you* to cherish yourself; and *Thank you* to acknowledge with gratitude who you are, the circumstances you are in, or the wonder and awe of just being alive.

5. **Connect with others.** Community nourishes you. You get a reflection of the positive impact you have, and begin to see how your life touches others. Prioritize spending time with people who love you in a supportive, easy way.

37

See your loved ones
with fresh eyes

Spark wonder and joy with a Beginner's Mind

· ·

"It is only with the heart that one can see rightly; what is essential is invisible to the eye."

—Antoine de Saint-Exupery, writer, pioneering aviator

The impact of mindfulness on relationships is always a popular topic among my corporate clients. To communicate this concept in our mindfulness training programs, we often ask people to face one another and look directly into each other's eyes for a brief moment—which can feel like an eternity. Intimacy can be scary, because it brings us closer to our more tender, vulnerable side. Yet everyone longs to be seen, to be recognized, to be known by other human beings—especially those we care about.

Being seen validates you. Seeing validates others. And when you see a person with clarity, the relationship gets real: A sense of safety develops and evokes an honest, authentic interaction. You affirm the person for who he or she is, not for what he or she has achieved or possesses.

But we aren't always seeing in the deepest sense of the word. Mindful "seeing" goes beyond sight to encompass the meaning in the words that a person speaks, the emotions that come from his or her expressions, the way he or she stands or moves—even the energy you pick up when that person is near. It may come as no surprise that mindful seeing can be hardest to achieve in our closest relationships.

Mindfulness can help you use this kind of seeing to deepen connections with others. It's too easy to develop a fixed view of who a loved one is, and time often narrows this perspective. We cling to our beliefs because, as humans, we like certainty; it's part of the brain's design that helps us conserve energy. But without updating our mental images, we miss how a loved one grows, how interests shift, and how personalities evolve. Mindfulness teaches impermanence: the recognition and acceptance that everything (and everyone) is constantly changing. Seeing your loved ones with fresh eyes—with the veils of old ideas and the glasses of yesterday's perceptions removed—allows for true connection.

How exactly do you look at your daily companions with a Beginner's Mind? You already understand that mindfulness can help you bring vivid awareness to what is right in front of you in any situation, including the familiar. Practicing openness and curiosity allows you to notice and appreciate the person who is with you *in that moment.* You might spot the tiny tattoo on your sister and inquire about the meaning. Or when your child explains what happened that hurt her feelings during the after-school club, you might recognize that she has an expanded sense of self. Or you might see anew your partner's witty sense of humor that initially attracted you, but has been lost in the day-to-day details of your busy lives.

Remember that how you see others also affects them. German author and statesman Johann Wolfgang von Goethe wrote, "The way you see people is the way you treat them, and the way you treat them is what they become." I see this so clearly in my own marriage. The first time I glimpsed the man who would later become my husband was on a white-water rafting trip at the mouth of the Youghiogheny River in Pennsylvania. He arrived wearing a denim shirt with mother-of-pearl snap buttons, well-cut jeans, and black leather wing-tip shoes, while the rest of us wore T-shirts and shorts over our bathing suits. He had just arrived in the United States from Germany, and his style, accent, and elegance were striking. It didn't take long for a relationship to develop, and our attraction was palpable: We even had a hand signal we gave each other—palms up by our eyes, fingers flashing open and closed, to say, *I see you with adoring eyes.* More than 20 years later, I still think my husband is hot, but he might not know it from my everyday glance. Our hand signal shows up less frequently; I often see him more as the co-manager of our home, my partner in parenting, my financial adviser in growing my company. But when I choose to open my eyes and see him "freshly"—I see the strong lines of his face, his sparkling eyes, his elegant way of standing, his strength, his kind actions—it's a way of sustaining and nourishing our loving connection.

Seeing people fully is what Thich Nhat Hanh calls "Looking Deeply"— nonjudgmentally directing your attention to the present moment and the person who is in it with you. One smart way to look deeply comes from California mindfulness educator Mitra Manesh. She uses a technique she calls Living Portraits, in which two people gaze at each other with kindness and curiosity, as if each person were a work of art. The goal is to peer into the life journey that each has lived: the sadness, the joys, the moments of hope. Try looking at someone you love with all of your senses in this way. You can also try imagining his or her happiest moments as a child: playing, running, laughing. Your own joyful spirit will connect with the same joyful spirit in that person, creating a moment of wonder and love. Seeing each other in this way will not only cultivate intimacy, but also nourish you *and* your partner.

How: •

1. **Look deeply into the eyes.** Be brave. It takes courage to really look at another, not as a staring contest, but as a way to go through the "doorway to the soul" of the person who is with you now.

2. **Recognize and reflect.** See others with an open mind. Let the recognition of the person you are with be reflected in your eyes, in your facial expression, and in how you hold your body.

3. **Speak from your heart.** Say what you see in those you love. Be a mirror for them, allowing them to more clearly see themselves.

4. **Allow yourself to be seen.** Remove your protective layers; if you're sad, take off the mask of good cheer. Honor the limited time we have with each other with authenticity.

5. **Notice the impact.** Tune in to your feelings as you see someone you love in a present, fresh, curious way. Observe how this kind of seeing changes the interaction—and even the relationship—over time.

38

Forgive from the heart

*Use understanding, empathy, and acceptance
to open your heart so you can forgive*

. . . .

"Human beings, by changing the inner attitudes of their minds, can change the outer aspects of their lives."

—William James, philosopher, psychologist

Forgiveness is a critical part of navigating relationships and taking care of your heart with mindful compassion. But it doesn't come easily.

In the coastal redwoods of California, Buddhist author and teacher Jack Kornfield taught a group of us mindfulness teachers that forgiveness is a fierce practice. You must be willing to face what is difficult, to step into a swamp of deep sorrow and even grief at times. Refusing to forgive is a form of resistance to life—it's the opposite of acceptance. It creates and maintains an internal struggle that can feel like contraction, tightness, and heaviness in your body. It's a hard load to travel with, especially in the realm of our closest relationships.

Forgiveness means freedom from carrying around the endless ruminations, blame, resentments, anger, and even rage. And that freedom opens the way to understanding—something that Thich Nhat Hanh sees as central to love. He believes that "understanding is love's other name."

To love someone means to open your heart to sensing what is causing the other person emotional or physical pain, which Buddhists call suffering. Nhat Hanh teaches that although we all long to be understood, fear, insecurity, and unwillingness to be vulnerable to more pain can block our ability to leap across the walls we erect between each other.

But mindfulness can help us clear the way to understanding. It starts with acceptance. By acknowledging the truth of a situation, you activate a higher level of thinking and widen perspective. That doesn't mean you should condone harmful behavior—but taking a minute to separate biases from reality can give you the space to respond with courage, intelligence, and compassion. Acceptance connects you with your deepest, wisest loving self—even in the face of strong emotions.

After acceptance, you can move forward with cognitive empathy and understanding. Ask yourself questions about the person you intend to forgive: What conditions in his or her own childhood might have led to a particular behavior? What experiences of suffering could have led your offender to this act that hurt you? What were the stressors and conditions of his or her life when this happened? These questions are not about condoning, but instead about creating more space for understanding. Curiosity and openness allow us to move past our strong positions and assumptions, increasing our ability to see from another person's perspective.

We can all do this. Scientists have concluded that humans are born wired for empathy, which is the capacity to sense other people's emotions. Have you ever made faces at a baby and watched him or her mirror your expressions? Scientists at the University of Parma found that babies as young as nine months old can mimic the expressions of another human being. Researchers also know that the more you see that others are similar to you, the more empathy you are able to feel. Empathy lays the groundwork for compassion, which is the recognition of suffering and the wish to see that suffering relieved. You can strengthen your empathy in forgiveness situations with the Just Like Me practice, saying phrases such as *Just like me, he is also a human being who is doing the best he can. Just like me, he makes mistakes. Just like me, she also has room for healing and growth.*

And then practicing loving-kindness with phrases such as *I wish for her to find peace. May he feel understood and loved.*

Like physical therapy after an injury, forgiveness after a hurt can take repeated practice and time. Psychologist and mindfulness teacher Tara Brach emphasizes that forgiveness is usually a gradual, emotional process—not something the mind takes on purely by thinking. It requires that you move closer to your suffering. When you've been wounded, you cannot just decide that you "should" forgive the other person. Moving forward in this process requires a compassionate attention to your own heart; in some cases, you need to forgive yourself. You can do that by calming your body with your breath, putting your hand on your own heart, and saying, *Forgiven, forgiven.* Give it time, and allow the gradual process of forgiveness to unfold, uncovering a larger, more compassionate part of yourself that can hold wounds with love. Once you've treated yourself with a gentle kindness, it is possible to widen the circle of compassion to include another.

How:

1. **Acknowledge and accept the hurt.** Bring mindful compassion to yourself for feeling hurt, betrayal, disappointment, or grief from losing something you once had. Sense where you feel the hurt in your body, then breathing softly, let yourself feel the walls you have built and the emotional pain of keeping your heart closed.

2. **Be curious and open.** Mindfulness trains you to let go of judgment, which promotes understanding. Look at what's underneath on both sides, such as fears, attachments, and needs. Acknowledge the longing for love as a central need.

3. **Access empathy and practice compassion for your offender.** Use the phrase "Just like me" to train yourself to see the commonality of our human experience and the similarities you share with your offender. Ask yourself about the suffering and conditions that might have led to your offender's behavior, to allow yourself to understand the vulnerability of being human.

4. **Allow forgiveness to flow from compassion.** Send loving-kindness wishes to the other person: *I hope she will feel understood* or *I hope he finds peace in our relationship.* You can start with the universal wish to avoid pain and access love. And it's okay if you are not ready to forgive just yet. Remember forgiveness takes time.

5. **Communicate with truth.** Choosing honesty instead of masking, denying, or withholding the truth will lead to understanding. Moreover, it will strengthen trust and intimacy with the other person.

6. **Forgive yourself.** Use the same steps of cognitive understanding, acceptance, and compassion with yourself. Using a gentle touch on your arm or your heart to calm your body, actively forgive yourself when you need to by breathing deeply and saying, *All is okay; you are forgiven.*

7. **Find meaning and purpose in your suffering.** These experiences make you more sensitive to others' pain, and can give you opportunities to help others who are hurting, or motivate you to prevent others from suffering similar injustices.

39

Choose generosity

Generosity is love in action

. . . .

"Love and generosity creates an exchange of positive energy, and fuels further love and generosity."

—Sharon Salzberg, author, meditation teacher

Richard Davidson, founder of the Center for Healthy Minds in Madison, Wisconsin, teaches that generosity is one of four pillars of well-being (the others being attention, resilience, and a positive outlook). Davidson points to research showing that altruistic behavior can actually activate key positive emotions in the brain and body. So how do we use that insight in daily life?

Like many people, you might think of generosity as making a donation to a charity at the end of the year, giving gifts to relatives and friends on your holiday list, or maybe volunteering at your child's school. You probably don't think of generosity as a formidable strategy for transforming how you relate to others, to yourself, and to the world. But the truth is that generosity is a superpower: It can reach into your core and loosen the grip of fear or override feelings of weakness or inadequacy.

Generosity grows from a sense of abundance, a willingness to open up and share what you have. When you are able to part with things, time, or ideas—transforming what you once saw as "mine" and accept them as "ours"—you tap into a potent source of strength, freedom, and happiness. You can find opportunities to be generous in all areas of life: when you receive an email from a co-worker asking for help, when you walk by a homeless person in need, when a friend asks for your advice, or when a loved one needs your affection. Norwegian poet Arne Garborg captures this beautifully: "To love someone is to learn the song in their heart and sing it to them when they have forgotten."

Forgiving someone is also an act of generosity, and studies show that the positive feelings it generates in the forgiver can reduce stress and sadness and lead to lower heart rates and blood pressure.

At key points throughout the day you have the option to dedicate your time, resources, ideas, or love—and yet sometimes, we still look the other way. Maybe it's a trade-off mindset: *I will give this amount or this gift if I am appreciated for this act of giving.* One of my clients, a businessman in Chicago, told me he routinely thinks, *If I give an hour to my relatives, will it cut into my "me" time? If I donate money to my kid's school, will I lose out on something else?* But the good news is that simply being conscious of these tendencies—noticing when you hesitate or decline to give—is a way toward different choices. Mindfulness helps you see what you are attached to and what motivates you, and creates space for you to take control and nudge yourself toward generosity.

Being generous is a practice that can help define who you are—but keep in mind that you actually have to practice it. According to sociologists who study the effects of generosity, this action has to be sustained over time to become a trait. My mother was an example of this: She volunteered every Wednesday night in the church kitchen preparing meals for young people with special needs until the last week of her life. The night of her stroke, she had spent the evening taking ladies who didn't drive to a Thursday night holy service before Easter. She made generosity a way of life.

Generosity is a visible affirmation of human connectedness. In its truest form, it isn't based on whether someone deserves kindness, and it isn't expecting anything in return. And yet what it creates is invaluable.

How:

1. **Be present for loved ones.** The greatest gift you can offer anyone you love is your presence, according to Thich Nhat Hanh. Before you spend time with a loved one, close your eyes, breathe, and allow your body to settle, letting go of any stress or tightness. Now you are ready to be fully there for your companion.

2. **Listen generously.** Pay attention with an open mind and genuine interest. Make time and space to take in not only the content of the spoken words, but also the feelings and emotions of the speaker.

3. **Embrace gratitude.** Make a list once a week of things you are grateful for and why they matter. Focusing on what you have instead of what you don't will build a sense of abundance and make it much easier for you to be generous with others in all aspects of your life.

4. **Give your time.** Align your skills and strengths with your community's needs. Volunteer at a school, cook a meal, mentor someone who is learning. Every small act counts—holding the door, carrying groceries, fixing a neighbor's car.

5. **Generate positive thoughts.** Make it a habit to be generous in how you think about others. Counter your tendency to judge or compare others with focusing on the good in each person you encounter—especially your loved ones. Express appreciation specifically and frequently; send "thank you" notes, emails, texts—whatever gets the message across.

40

Touch with presence

Tune in to your direct experience of making physical contact

· ·

"To touch can be to give life."

—Michelangelo, artist

Humans need touch to thrive, yet many of us are starved for it—not only because we don't touch enough, but also because we don't bring an alert, mindful presence to the interaction. I speak from experience. One Sunday afternoon while our daughter was at a birthday party, my husband and I faced one another in the quiet of our bedroom. We were there physically, but my mind was elsewhere—I was trying to remember the last time we had a Sunday afternoon encounter, and why it was so long ago. Then my mind turned to all the errands I still needed to run that day, and to the pickup time for the birthday party. It's natural for our minds to be always generating thoughts, yet I was missing what could be a special moment of connection. Suddenly, the words "direct experience" popped into my head. The phrase led me back to the person in front of me. I placed a hand on my husband's shoulder, noticing the warmth and softness of the skin. Tuning in to the range of sensations I felt, I was completely there for him.

Physical contact is not only about mindfully giving, but also mindfully receiving. Touch is a bilateral highway. To make the most of any exchange—whether it's holding hands, hugging, or something more intimate—use mindful breathing to bring you to the present. Then pay attention to the physical sensations, emotions, and thoughts that arise for you with touch. Make an effort to do so without judgment. In time, this awareness can help you intensify the way you interact and communicate—and ultimately boost your connection and enjoyment.

In addition to heightening awareness—and desire—touching someone you love can actually reduce stress. And the stronger the partnership, the more powerful the effect. A groundbreaking 2006 study, published in the journal *Psychological Science,* found that married women under extreme stress who were able to hold their husbands' hands felt immediate relief. The study used an fMRI machine to scan 16 happily married women in their 30s as they were warned that they were about to get a series of small electric shocks to their ankle. While awaiting the shocks, the participants' brains showed peaks of activation in regions involved in anticipating pain, increasing physical arousal, and regulating negative emotions, among other systems. But the moment the women felt their husbands' hands (while still in the machine), their brain scans looked calmer. In comparison tests, holding a stranger's hand had more of an effect than holding no hand, but a husband's touch provided the greatest relief by far. Furthermore, the wives in the happiest marriages (based on a survey the couples filled out beforehand) had the calmest brains under stress.

But you don't need an MRI machine to discover the benefits of touch. Hugs and massage are two other forms of contact that are easy to come by, and can have big payoffs for health and well-being—not to mention love. Research shows that getting five hugs a day for four weeks increases happiness—most likely because a hug, especially a long one, releases oxytocin (aka the "love" hormone). A short massage can provide a similar lift. My husband and I use massage with our daughter before bed to soothe her and ease her growing pains. We often use it on each other as part of our end-of-day mindfulness routine. It only takes 10 minutes of massage, studies show, to improve sleep and reduce fatigue (touch increases the neurotransmitters serotonin and dopamine and decreases the stress hormone cortisol). A shoulder rub can be a quick pick-me-up at any time of day, or a mini-mindfulness practice of intentional generosity and love when someone around you needs it.

How:

1. **Designate time for touch.** Align your time with what matters most. If you live with a partner, schedule regular rendezvous. If you live alone, book an appointment to get or give a massage.

2. **Infuse touch with intention.** Take the time to direct your body with purpose. If you share your intention first, you help the receiver to be more open and aware: *I'm going to massage your shoulders to relax you and show you how much I appreciate you.*

3. **Make touching a mindfulness practice.** Slowly move your hand around your partner's body, focusing on the point of contact and using your breath to stay in the present. Let intuition guide how you touch, and tune in to your partner for cues. When distractions hijack your concentration, bring your mind back to the points of physical contact with your partner.

4. **Touch others more.** Whether it's a touch on the arm, a gentle pat on the back, or a hand on the shoulder, practice making contact with acquaintances when appropriate. Give more hugs and massages, being fully present when you do.

41

Gather your posse

*Come together in community with rituals and traditions
to nourish and deepen your mindfulness practice*

• •

"Let us imagine the care of the soul, then, as an application of poetics
to everyday life."

—Thomas Moore, monk, author

Ping! On Sunday nights at 6:30 p.m., my mobile phone and laptop
send a reminder. A written message appears that says, "Family *sangha*
in 30 minutes." I have time to mindfully prepare—to gather the round
silver tray, a candle, our small gold mindfulness bell on its purple
cushion, a favorite mindfulness book, and to make some tea in a beautiful iron teapot. I light the candle, and my husband, daughter, and I
sit on floor cushions around the silver tray. It might sound cliché, but
we like to light incense as well, because the wafting smoke is another
cue to relax, tune in with all our senses, and just come home to being
with each other.

We gather each Sunday evening to simply be in each other's presence,
with mindfulness. Different from family game night or dinner together,
the intention is that we see one another, breathe together, strengthen our
connection, and express appreciation. One way we do that is by what

Thich Nhat Hanh calls "watering each other's flowers." When we water the flowers of another, we share specific moments of appreciation about something that person did that week or a quality about that person. Ava Grace might say, "Mom, thank you for taking me and my friends to the movies, and for not getting upset when I lost my new jacket." I might tell my husband that I appreciate his steady calm during our busy week, and for the delicious dinner he prepared for our dinner party. After watering flowers, we sometimes clear the air of anything hurtful or regretful that might have come up during the week with another practice called "Beginning Anew." Andreas could say, "Laurie, when you changed our dinner plans because something else came up, I was disappointed and a little mad." This gives us a chance to bring things into the light and treat them with tenderness and compassion, rather than let unpleasant feelings smolder and build up. It also makes loving communication a norm. We have adapted rituals and practices we learned on our family mindfulness retreats, but you can organize your own gatherings of family, friends, or whatever mix of people you like. It's an act of love to create conditions for people to come together and connect in meaningful, nourishing ways.

Gathering with intention to connect and practice rituals, often referred to broadly as contemplative practices, is by no means new, but there does seem to be a need now more than ever to create these sacred spaces with others in our lives. A 2004 report by Massachusetts' Center for Contemplative Mind in Society noted that "a renaissance is under way to apply the contemplative disciplines to the rhythm of our everyday lives—lives spent in offices, classrooms, courtrooms, and living rooms." Regular gatherings are a long-standing spiritual tradition, from the Jewish Shabbat dinner on Friday nights to Christian church services on Sunday mornings. When I was in high school I hosted a Friday morning prayer group in my home with my teenage friends. In the Buddhist tradition, a *sangha* is a local community of mindfulness practitioners who gather to meditate, to share their joys and difficulties, and to encourage each other on the path of practice. Our family created a sangha for the weekly mindfulness gathering in our living room, but it doesn't matter what you call it. Just set the intention to bring people together—daily, weekly, monthly, or whatever works—with the purpose of deepening presence and connection.

Be open to what form your gathering might take. You can make it a tea-infused meditation and gratitude evening like ours—or depending on your group, you can adapt it to your favorite ways of being mindful. In a recent two-day Search Inside Yourself program I taught in Copenhagen, one of the participants decided to convert the monthly Saturday morning hikes she organizes into mindful hikes, where the group starts with a few minutes of mindful breathing and then enjoys nature together.

On a recent walk, I saw something overhead that reminded me of sangha: a flock of geese flying in a V formation. It was the picture of community, much like what we can create in our "mindfulness tribes." Like birds flying together, ". . . the presence of others lends power to your wings during this journey across the sky of life," writes Madisyn Taylor, founder of *DailyOM,* an inspirational website. The birds' alignment also reminded me that we are all connected at the deepest levels—supported, protected, and led forward by each other. It is up to you to intentionally gather your tribe to cultivate community and connection—one of the greatest sources of joy and well-being.

How:

1. **Seek out others.** Establish connections with friends, family, and others who are exploring mindfulness practices, and invite them to gather. We all long to belong.

2. **Designate a place, day, and time to come together.** It can be weekly, monthly—whatever works. You can make this a routine, or host mindful gatherings intermittently.

3. **Create rituals and routines.** Use this book and other favorites to create a template for your own sangha with family or friends. Serve tea, practice mindful breathing together, read poetry or favorite passages, and use a mindfulness bell to open and close the gathering.

4. **Express appreciation.** In smaller gatherings, make time to share with each person what you appreciated about him or her this week. Make it specific. This is called "watering each other's flowers."

5. **Try the Beginning Anew practice.** In regular gatherings with family or close friends, you can use rituals to keep things clear. When hurts or misunderstandings have come up during the week, create a regular time in your gathering to give space to allow these to surface with mindful listening, be greeted with empathy and compassion, and heal and nourish the relationship.

6. **Take turns.** Rotate who does what: One person makes and serves the tea, another sounds the bell, a third chooses a poem passage or uplifting story to read. This works well when children are present. Give everyone a part to enhance the connection.

42

Be open to grief

*Mindfulness skills help you deal with the hardest part of love,
which is loss*

· ·

"Love is the root of all joy and sorrow."

—Meister Eckhart, philosopher

When I was living in San Francisco, nine months pregnant with my daughter, I had a strong sense that I should stay home instead of going into the office one Tuesday morning. My team was waiting for me, and I felt fine, so it was unusual for me to choose this course. An hour later, I received a call from my mother. My 37-year-old brother Johnny had died unexpectedly.

I felt as if I were floating out of my body. I was in a numb fog, yet I also had a heightened sense of alertness and clarity. I could see sharply, but I *felt* disoriented—like a significant physical part of me was missing.

Our natural tendency is to withdraw from pain—physical *and* emotional—and sometimes that can help. And, sometimes, we manage pain by "compartmentalizing"—deciding that the hurt does not have to affect every area of our life. Wharton professor Adam Grant shared this healthy strategy with his friend and Facebook COO, Sheryl Sandberg, when she had to face the sudden death of her husband in 2015. These gut reactions to stress might be a necessity, enabling us to harness available energy to do what needs to be done. It helped me when I had to go to the morgue, and to Johnny's apartment, and then arrange the details for getting his body home to my family in Maryland. I had to think about my husband and my baby and my job. I had to focus.

But compartmentalizing is at best a temporary refuge. Mindfulness is foundational. It can help you develop the capacity to face the pain of loss. By allowing you to notice the sensations present in your body—the emotions, the thoughts—you can then transform them into acceptance, letting go, and finally, peace.

In the weeks that followed losing Johnny, I started to open to the deep well of grief. I used mindful breathing to soothe myself when I felt a wave of emotion coming over me. A well-known Buddhist adage says, "It is not about denying or suppressing the emotion, but learning to surf the waves." Once I reached a calmer state through a few moments of focused breathing, I would do a mini-body scan, noting each physiological sensation. At first, I felt a dense, heavy weight in my chest and abdomen, and also a pervasive uneasiness. But just acknowledging and allowing these feelings to be there (I used the mantra, *Oh, this is here*) eventually gave them the space to rise and fall away.

As children, Johnny and I used to tell people that we were twins. Indeed, we always felt like soul mates. And in grieving, I found that the depth of my sadness was correlated to the depth of our love. It was the other side of the coin: love and loss, directly proportional. That realization represented a shift for me. Now, I could meet the waves of emotion from a broader field—not the pit of sadness, but the expansive sky of love. I felt connected with other families going through loss, and ultimately with all humans, because we all experience loss and pain. I learned to say to myself, *Oh, here is the love for Johnny welling up again.* I was able to allow all of it to be present—the sadness and the love.

Mindfulness practice trains you to "be here" with all emotions, instead of burying or denying them. This also works well for broken hearts. You might experience anger, sadness, guilt, or fear when a relationship ends.

And these feelings might be mixed with love, joy, pride, and happiness. You can allow sadness, but you can also allow the part of you that wants to resist sadness. Your awareness has room for all of the emotions—even the ones that seem to contradict each other. What matters is that you notice the range of feelings, and in doing so stay in touch with the entire scope of your existence. Then you can experience grief without being overwhelmed by it.

The second part of grieving is to strengthen resilience, which comes in part from how you interpret the loss. Mindful self-awareness means you're conscious of the frames and filters (mindsets, for example) through which you view your experiences. Some people tend to be optimists, some pessimists; some people see what happens from a victim's point of view—*Why did this happen to me?*—and others don't take events personally. What patterns do you notice in thinking about your loss? Instead of being caught in reactions, you can cultivate equanimity by letting go of what does not serve you: blame, anger, resistance. Treating yourself with kindness, reframing your perspective, and accepting your new reality are the pillars of strengthening resilience after a loss.

It takes courage and intention to alchemize negative feelings like sadness and despair into feelings of hope and love. In 2011, six weeks before my husband, daughter, and I were to move from Germany to the United States to live near my mother, she died suddenly from a stroke. I could not believe the timing. For years she had been asking us to bring her youngest granddaughter closer to her, and when I finally organized a new life in the States, Mom was gone. I wrestled with "if only" thoughts and torturous "woulda-shoulda-coulda" ruminations, which only deepened my pain. Buddhists call this the "second arrow"—the first arrow being the original pain, and the next being what hits us when we add to the pain with self-blame. I had to acknowledge and accept the truth of the moment I was in before I could move forward with self-compassion, and be able to rest in the love we shared.

Everything changes, including your experience with heartbreak and grief. And in time, I felt the physicality of grief moving from constriction in my chest to a lightness. I became freer to accept her death, to celebrate how my mother continues on in my daughter and me, and to allow her enduring love for me to give strength, peace, and joy.

How: ·

1. **Allow your emotions.** When experiencing the physical pain of loss, don't try to deny, suppress, or avoid it. Learn to stay and look at pain as something impermanent passing through your body.

2. **See your grief.** Recognize that this is how your life is right now—you navigating your broken or grieving heart. See what it feels like to simply let go of wishing life were different, and allow what is here to be here, just as it is.

3. **Connect with others.** Draw on the strength of others and let them be with you. Their presence can fortify you in the hard moments. Seek help from professionals when needed.

4. **Nourish with kindness.** Commit to self-care routines and medical appointments while grieving. Get massages, exercise, nutrition, and rest.

5. **Orient to the positive.** When you are ready, turn your mind to the good about the person you miss and the connection you shared. Recall positive qualities, beloved memories, and the experiences you shared, and how you accompanied one another in this life. See the sadness as an integral part of the love.

6. **Journal your experience.** Along with using expressive writing to let your feelings flow on the page, generate feelings of gratitude for sharing part of your life with your loved one. Try writing a letter to the person you lost, conveying all the love, joy, and gratitude you feel.

Home:
End the Day

A mindful end of day begins when you reenter your home after being out in the world. It's about *how* you come in to your space; *how* you maintain an abode that is nourishing and inspiring; and *how* you go about enjoying the moments in your evening instead of "getting through" the hours until you collapse into bed. A mindful evening has more to do with your state of "being" than with what you're actually "doing." Whether you're wrangling three young kids or preparing a solo dinner, you can practice mindfulness to wind down your day and enjoy your evening with intention and awareness—and joy.

By now you have a tool kit of strategies for cultivating calm and presence—but end-of-day exhaustion can tempt us to slip into autopilot. If your house is chaotic, returning from the office might feel like jumping out of the frying pan and into the fire. Or if your house is quiet, with everyone plugged in to their own devices, you might find it even harder to let go of tension from the day as your mind fills with its own noise of ruminating about the past and worrying about the future. In either case, mindfulness practices and kind attention can help. This final section offers repeatable, reliable ways for you to direct your mind to the good and ease your body toward sleep.

Being present for the last part of the day is as important as getting a strong start to the morning. It's not just setting yourself up for relaxation and enjoyment (though the benefits of sufficient rest are profound). At the end of even the most trying days, mindfulness can help you to remember who you are. Jon Kabat-Zinn describes it as a "re-membering": a coming back into your body and reengaging with your core values and desires, as well as the wishes of your heart. Your evenings are opportunities to reflect on who you want to be and the nourishing sanctuary you want to create, and to set and live from these intentions. Maybe you want to see your loved one with fresh eyes, or infuse more delight into your day by savoring a home-cooked meal. Whatever you do, taking back your evenings can quickly add up to taking back your life.

43

Transition peacefully from day to evening

Shift from busyness and stress to calm, clarity, and tranquility

· ·

"I have arrived, I am home."

—Thich Nhat Hanh, poet, peace activist, Zen master

My friend Krista is a public defender, triathlete, and mom to two grade-school girls. Like so many of us, she finds it difficult to unhook from her workday when she gets home. "The first thing I need to do is unload about my frustrations," Krista says of her struggle to relax into being with her family. I hear similar stories from many clients and friends.

All transitions can be difficult to navigate, but the shift from being out in the world to coming home each evening can be particularly stressful. Work, errands, commuting—whatever is on your schedule is likely to be full of logistical challenges, uncertainties, and demands, even when it's an activity of your choosing. It's easy to get caught up in the intensity and the energy of "doing" during your day, and hard to let go and come into the moment when you get home.

Consider your most recent return home: Did you walk through the door with your mind still replaying a scene from the day or ruminating about that last thing you couldn't check off your to-do list? As we've learned, this is natural, but it also takes a toll: Our worrying thoughts affect our bodies, our bodies affect our thoughts and emotions, and our emotions affect our experience, as well as those around us. And the cycle continues. When your body is already worn down from back-to-back meetings, too much caffeine, and not enough fresh air, it's even more important to know how to break through to ease and peace.

But it is possible. To start, track your transition for a week and notice how you come in the door. Maybe your tendency is to repress the hard stuff during the day, and then let it out in a burst when you get home, like Krista. Or maybe you constrict your body, moving with a tenseness and tightness to quietly carry the stress through the evening and into the next day. As you now know, these behaviors are rooted in the neurobiological response to stress—fight, flight, or freeze—but they can manifest differently for everyone. Bringing mindful awareness to your own patterns is the first step in freeing yourself from them.

Mindfulness provides a temperature gauge to assess where you are. As you start to integrate mindful pauses into your day, it will be easier to pause at the door and take a reading. You already know how to reflect on your mood with gentle awareness, observing your thoughts and emotions. And naming what's going on—*tired, frustrated, excited, hopeful, overwhelmed*—can help keep you from reacting instead. You can use this pause to read your own state, as well as to sense the emotional mood of others around you.

Remember that this transition will set the tone for the quality of your evening. And whether you spend your free time luxuriating in the peace and quiet of home, rejoicing in the madness that is life with kids, or savoring the company of a loved one, it beats losing your night to thoughts of the day behind or the day ahead. Rehashing the past and worrying about the future dims the vividness and joy available in the present. If enjoying personal time isn't enough motivation, bear in mind that your transition from work to home affects those around you, too. Being open, receptive, and present with your family, roommates, or friends is the best thing you can do for them—and yourself.

How: ···

1. **Speak your intention.** As you pull up in the car, take the elevator up to your floor, or put your hand on the doorknob, say out loud: *I am calm, peaceful, and present when I enter my home.*

2. **Use doors as cues.** When you pass through a door leaving work or cross the threshold into your home, let the exit or entryway serve as a "mindfulness bell" to remind you to pause for a moment and check in.

3. **Do a three-center check-in.** Pause and take three breaths to settle your mind and body. Use inquiry to investigate. **Head:** *What are my thoughts right now?* **Body:** *What sensations are present?* **Heart:** *What emotions are present?*

4. **Attend and befriend.** If you notice difficult emotions, such as anxiety, anger, sadness, or frustration, pause and bring loving attention to where you feel the emotion in the body. Send kindness to yourself, even talking to yourself as you would a friend. *Oh, you are still embarrassed about the meeting. You will be okay, sweetheart.*

5. **Listen mindfully.** If someone is at home when you arrive, notice if you feel an impulse to unload strong emotions or immediately debrief the day. Can you instead be a compassionate presence, listening without agenda, just being there for the other person?

6. **Orient to the positive.** Enjoy your evening by taking in the good. Offset your evolutionary negativity bias by directing your attention to what is going well in the moment. There is skill in choosing which seeds to water—the negative seeds or the positive seeds. It is *your* garden.

44

Clear your home for calm and joy

The state of your living space reflects you and affects you

• •

"We shape our dwellings, and afterwards our dwellings shape us."

—Winston Churchill, former British prime minister

What we learn as we become more mindful is that our internal environment affects our external world: our teams, our families, our relationships, even our physical space. I have a card from Thich Nhat Hanh in my kitchen that says, "Peace in oneself, peace in the world." The internal affects the external, but the reverse is also true: The external affects the internal. Your environment can influence your state of being. Can you recall being in a place of serenity and beauty, such as a museum, a courtyard or a back porch with an exceptional view? How did you feel there—in your body, your breathing, your feelings and thoughts? Curating your home to match your intentions for how you want to live your life—with calm, joy, creativity, connection, or whatever you seek—can help you cultivate those qualities.

If you're at home or in your office, look around. Does your space nourish and ground you, or does it feel cluttered and suffocating? A lot of people might identify more with the latter; Americans and other cultures have a complicated relationship with "things," and it's common to feel the need to surround ourselves with material stuff whether or not we really want it. For me, the habit comes from my parents' postwar mindset. Nothing was ever thrown away; an item could always be repaired, repurposed, or reused. My four siblings and I grew up in a house brimming with knickknacks, travel souvenirs, and handcrafted gifts that we had made for our mom and dad. I've mostly moved away from this tendency to accumulate—but decades later, I still find myself fighting an inner voice (surely my mother's) that says, *Save this, you might need it someday.*

The attitudes of mindfulness—impermanence, letting go, gratitude, and generosity—guide me in deciding what to keep and what to shed. In fact, those concepts steered me through the ultimate organizational project: going through the belongings of my mom, dad, and brothers after their deaths at different times. I was face-to-face with life's impermanence—but that reality helped push me to say goodbye to tangible objects and reconnect with what really mattered during our time together.

I have maintained that discerning attitude in my own home—particularly after living in northern Europe, where most rooms are spare and only beloved objects are displayed. I also appreciate the inspiration from the Japanese tidying expert and best-selling author Marie Kondo. Kondo's practices are simple but effective, and dovetail perfectly with the mindful practices of this book. In *The Life-Changing Magic of Tidying Up*, Kondo details her method of considering each object in a home: taking a moment to connect with it, and then deciding if it "sparks joy" or not. If the book, piece of clothing, or kitchen utensil gives you a good vibe, keep it. If not, let it go, Kondo suggests. Her process is much like the mindful practice STOP, in which you **s**top, **t**ake a breath, direct attention to the **o**bject and **o**bserve the thoughts and emotions that arise. Last is **p**roceed—in this case, choosing to keep the object in its place or giving it away.

Kondo also has a brilliant application of gratitude in her organizational method: She suggests saying, "Thank you" to a possession for its service before parting with it. It might sound odd, but the small act allows you to appreciate that the object fulfilled its purpose in a certain time and place, and is no longer needed. I expand on this with the belief that generosity empowers us to move things forward. Viewing these objects as gifts to others who can use them now is a satisfying way to complete this process.

Finally, I honor what I do decide to keep. I treasure the boxes filled with keepsakes, letters, and other mementos that celebrate each family member. When I look at those contents or share them with someone close to me, it sparks joy and love.

Safeguard similar treasures: things that speak to your heart and happiness. And before you begin to root out all the rest, create a vision for your ideal home. Cultivate your own style, paying attention to color, textures, and design elements that inspire you. Embrace your unique preferences and remember that as long as your space reflects the positive mood you want to foster, you cannot go wrong. During my years abroad, I found serenity and joy in the homes of friends in Germany, Denmark, and Switzerland, and have designed my current home to reflect those qualities with minimal decor and maximum beauty: airy, light spaces; bare wooden floors; white walls and open shelves that leave all the attention to beloved art pieces, books, and furniture. My home sparks joy every day, and yours can too.

Try tending your home as you would a garden, moving from room to room and corner to corner to help each area to bloom to its full potential. The process alone can help you "wake up" to your home so that you start to notice and appreciate details that will help you enjoy *your* special sanctuary. When you return home after a busy day, respect your space by putting things away and making room for renewal. Treat it as a tangible expression of your mindful life—and see how the inner and outer harmony inspires you.

How:

1. **Have a vision.** Imagine your dream home, and don't hold back. Forget worries about budget and logistics—this is a fun exercise to help you picture the place that reflects who you are and how you want to live.

Notice any recurring themes in the colors, shapes, and structural design elements, and then see what you can make a reality. Modify as needed!

2. **Simplify your space.** Let go of things that don't spark joy. Ask yourself: *Is it useful? Is it beautiful? Does it have meaning in my life today?* Tune in to the sensations in your body as you hold the object. If the reaction is positive, keep it. If not, let it go.

3. **Make conscious choices.** Think before you buy, collect, or say "yes" to free offers. Does the item enhance your vision of home, or is it another item that will collect dust and take up space? If it's the latter, you know what to do.

4. **Have a place for everything.** When you come home in the evening, spend a few minutes putting things in their place with gratitude and care. The act of tidying can be rewarding—both as a fulfilled responsibility and as a step toward maximum relaxation and enjoyment in a soothing environment.

45

Cultivate hygge at home

Bring a mindful attention and purposeful action to creating conditions for warmth, coziness, and togetherness

. . . .

"The most important hour is always the present. The most significant person is the precisely the one sitting across from you right now. The most necessary work is always love."

—Meister Eckhart, philosopher

The Danes know a thing or two about long nights. With freezing temperatures and up to 17 hours of darkness a day in the depths of winter, people are forced to find comfort indoors. And that's where *hygge* (pronounced HOO-gah) comes in. The word is most often translated as coziness, but the sentiment is more nuanced than that. Hygge is about embracing the darkness instead of resisting it. It's about creating warmth and togetherness and basking in that experience. In *The Little Book of Hygge,* Meik Wiking calls it "coziness of the soul."

My years living in northern Germany finally helped me understand this concept. When the sun would set at 4 p.m., not to be seen again until 8 a.m., I would fight the darkness by turning on every lamp and overhead light in my apartment. A wise neighbor came to the rescue by modeling her version of hygge—or gemütlichkeit, as it's known in

Germany—and showing me how to savor the season instead of resisting it. That meant swapping the bright lights for candles, arranging pillows and furniture to draw family and friends close, and setting up comfortable nooks for relaxing. In Denmark and Germany alike, the concept of coziness is about being in the present and letting your surroundings nourish you.

But you don't necessarily need candles to make this happen. In *The Book of Hygge: The Danish Art of Contentment, Comfort, and Connection*, Louisa Thomsen Brits refers to this practice as a "life art," explaining that it's a devotion to making life enjoyable. The intention to create well-being for yourself and others pulls you out of your own thoughts and into the moment—and that act nudges you toward contentment in itself. It's a way of bringing meaning to our lives and making our own light, so to speak.

Develop your own rituals to promote hygge: Share a pot of tea with co-workers at the end of a hard day. Play board games with friends on Friday nights. Instead of eating while standing at the kitchen counter, put a vase of flowers on the table, sit down, and take time to taste every bite of your meal. Go for a Sunday afternoon or evening walk with family and friends—a traditional hygge ritual in northern European cultures. Our family likes to huddle close by a crackling fire; we wrap ourselves in sheepskin blankets and linger for hours. A neighbor of ours in Germany makes a ritual of "lighting the rooms" after the sun sets, consciously creating a warm glow and welcoming ambiance in preparation for the arrival of his wife and daughter.

Whatever you do to cultivate warmth, intimacy, and connection is a purposeful action that can boost your spirit and increase your well-being year-round.

How: ●

1. **Create hygge lighting.** Light candles nightly—don't wait for a special event. (There's a reason that tea lights and candles are more affordable at IKEA—the Swedes are hygge masters and recognize the value of

stocking up.) Experiment with using smaller lamps and soft lighting instead of fluorescent ceiling lights, and see how it affects the room.

2. **Think of the well-being of others.** Be aware of what those around you need. Could an extra pillow make your partner more comfortable? Could you invite your neighbor who's been too busy to cook over for dinner, or gather friends for evening drinks in the garden to revel in nice weather? Look for ways that you can add warmth or cheer to someone's day.

3. **Develop rituals.** Intentional routines can prompt you to slow down and relish certain feelings. Drinking hot cocoa after a day of play in the snow is a ritual to promote childlike joy and togetherness. Reading a favorite story aloud can have the same effect. Make a list of five hygge habits that you can turn to when you need a lift.

4. **Capture hygge through cooking.** Certain foods are associated with coziness, like freshly baked bread, a winter stew, or homemade pizza. Plan dinners that are sure to send comforting aromas wafting from the kitchen.

5. **Light a fire.** Whether a simple candle or a full-fledged bonfire, flames draw people close and deepen connection. And the warmth and good conversation can keep people lingering for hours.

6. **Ditch electronics.** Put away your phone, turn off the TV, and tune in to your surroundings to truly experience hygge. Create some tech-free times in your home to foster mindful connection.

7. **Foster togetherness without drama.** Discuss politics another day. Avoid bragging, boasting, or competing. Being together as "we" is more important than "me." Recall happy times together, and tell stories that reinforce your bond.

46

Cook with your senses

*Turn the daily act of preparing food into an opportunity
to train in mindfulness and increase joy*

• •

**"Cooking creates a sense of well-being for yourself and the people you
love and brings beauty and meaning to everyday life."**
— Alice Waters, chef, pioneer of the farm-to-table movement

I will never forget my experience in an old stone Tuscan house on a late
afternoon in Italy. One summer, a fellow consultant at Accenture invited
my family to visit him in Siena, where his family has lived for generations.
Stefano led us into the rustic stone kitchen, where a cook was placing
slices of bread over a grill in a large open fireplace. I sipped a glass of wine
that Stefano's uncle had made from their own grapevines while we
watched the bread crisp. The cook took the bread from the fire, rubbed
the pieces with a garlic clove, drizzled homemade olive oil, sprinkled juicy
red tomato over the top, and then handed a piece to each of us. Every
sense in my body was stimulated. The crunch, the aroma, the tastes
swirling in my mouth, the sounds in the kitchen—it was a moment of
heightened awareness.

Not every meal can be in an Italian kitchen, but you can elevate your
own cooking experience with mindfulness. Remember how you learned

to bring a Beginner's Mind to your daily commute and use your senses as you travel. The same principles apply to preparing food—particularly after a long day of work, when cooking might seem like a task to get through, rather than a pleasure. Slowing down to fully appreciate the ingredients, time, and effort that goes into your meal can pull you out of autopilot and into the rich experience that food offers.

Begin by activating your senses as you select ingredients: sniffing the sweet basil leaf, sampling the creamy dressing, noticing the smooth texture of the bell pepper or the feel of uncooked rice grains in your hand. Maintain that heightened awareness as you mix and combine foods, hearing the pop and hiss of olive oil hitting the pan, feeling the heat rise to warm your face, and maybe savoring the smooth taste of wine you drink while you work. If you'll be sharing your meal with others, invite them to join you in the preparation process. Talk about your favorite flavors, try new techniques, laugh about your slipups—whatever keeps your focus on the wonderful and nourishing act of making something to eat together.

Bring mindfulness to serving the food, too. Use the act of setting the table as a reminder to pause and check in with how you feel. Are you anxious about whether your family or guests will like the food? Scolding yourself because the chicken was on the grill too long? If discouraging thoughts are swirling, you know what to do by now. Take a mindful pause. Notice, breathe, reset. Then, with gratitude, take in the fresh, flavorful, colorful ingredients available to you and the joy of creatively putting them together. Appreciate the care you put into feeding yourself and others, and appreciate the people with whom you'll share the meal. If you're dining alone, maybe you can bring someone special to mind who's not there—your grandfather whose recipe you've made, or your best friend's method for dicing an onion without making your eyes water. Rest your mind in being grateful for the energy and dedication of the farmers that grew the food, the sellers who provided it to you. We're all interconnected.

When I cherish the good in the entire cooking experience, I'm again reminded of Italy. Over dozens of years in Tuscany in our family summer house, I learned from watching the locals approach cooking as both play and a way of expressing creativity and love. They hug their guests, engage in lively conversation, laugh freely, and delight in the wonder of their food—from fleshy figs and savory olives plucked from backyard trees to sun-ripened tomatoes to earthy porcini mushrooms foraged from the forest—before they even take the first bite. Whether you're a stellar chef or just learning your way around the kitchen, whether your ingredients come from your own garden or the corner market, mindfulness and savoring can make cooking a source of joy and connection for you, too.

How:

1. **Select ingredients with care.** When strolling the grocery stores, visiting a local farm, or rummaging through your refrigerator, look closer at produce and other fresh foods. Notice details, mentally describing them to yourself: crisp lettuce leaves, a firm cucumber, bright orange melon.

2. **Tune in to every step.** Pay attention as you chop, dice, and slice. (Your focus especially pays off when you're wielding a well-honed chef's knife!) As you add each ingredient in a recipe, see, smell, feel, hear, and taste. Marvel in the alchemy of blending.

3. **Use heat as an anchor.** From the moment you pour oil into a sauté pan, turn on the outdoor grill, or place water on the stove to boil in a pasta pot, listen to the sounds, feel the warmth, and enjoy the aromas that follow. If you get distracted, notice and bring yourself back to those sensations.

4. **Notice where your attention is.** Most meals require you to monitor multiple things at a time. While the pasta is boiling and the veggies are sizzling in the pan, keep a calm, centered presence. Don't get lost in thought, but pay attention to the tasks at hand. You can always recenter by paying attention to just one breath. Allow yourself to be present with the different physical senses—and if you get distracted, simply bring your attention back to these sounds and smells.

5. **Observe your emotions.** When cooking for others, notice the patterns that come up for you. Do you get tense while balancing the various

elements? Simply allow emotions to rise and fall—it only takes 90 seconds—and turn your attention to the sights, smells, and other sensations of the food.

6. **Practice a positive outlook.** Is your inner critic onto you for falling short of your idea of the perfect dinner party? Orient your mind to the delight available in cooking. Involve your guests and invoke a sense of play. Notice the mindsets that come up for you as you approach each task, and practice shifting to wonder, gratitude, and joy.

47

Savor eating

Bring awareness and joy to this fundamental part of your day

. . . .

"One of the very nicest things about life is the way we must regularly stop whatever it is we are doing and devote our attention to eating."

—Luciano Pavarotti, tenor

As we discovered in cooking with the senses, mindfulness can shift an experience from ordinary to revelatory. And when it comes to eating, you need nothing more than your appetite and a single food item. I like a good orange.

I'll share a favorite scenario, and then you might try closing your eyes and imagining a similar experience. On a warm summer night, I find a fresh orange in my fruit bowl and carry it out to the front porch. I notice the vivid color of the rind as I slowly start to peel. I inhale its sweet citrusy scent as I separate the segments, and let the sticky juice squirt onto my fingers. A few seeds break free and land on the wooden table below. I feel my mouth water, anticipating the first bite. Then I pop in a piece, and bite into it with intentional curiosity and wonder. Sensations of juiciness, tartness, and sweetness burst, and the intensity makes me feel refreshed and alive. It's as if this is the first orange I've ever eaten.

When I teach people to breathe mindfully, I point out that each breath has an inhale, an exhale, and a space between the breaths. You can apply that pattern to taking a bite: Every bite has a beginning, middle, and end—the first taste as it lands on your tongue, the confluence of flavors as you chew, and the interesting flavors that linger in your mouth. Break down the parts of a bite as a way to deepen your attention and help you notice the details of what you're eating.

There's more to mindful eating than flavor. Consume with reverence and gratitude for all of the natural elements and human hands that helped bring the food to the table. You can make this a habit through the ritual of saying grace. In Japan, people say *"Itadakimasu"* ("I humbly receive") in unison before a meal. At Thich Nhat Hanh's meditation centers, the following statement is repeated before meals: *This food is a gift of the earth, the sky, numerous living beings, and much hard and loving work.* Whatever words you choose, the act of giving thanks out loud will reinforce the sentiment and elevate the experience.

I'll be the first to admit that it can be hard to maintain focus throughout a meal. Even at the table or countertop, distractions vie for your attention. But here's a profound mindfulness lesson I have learned while at monasteries: When you're eating, just eat. When you're drinking, just drink. If it sounds oversimplified, try it and see what I mean. Hide your phone, turn off the television, and tune in to your food, just as I described with the orange. Don't let eating be a chore to get through, or something you do "on the side" while you're at your desk or reading the paper (remember multitasking?). Food can be one of life's deepest pleasures if you approach it with all of your senses and give it the honored place in your day it deserves—and that *you* deserve. Nourish yourself with not just *what* you eat but *how* you eat, and you will invite pure joy into your life at least three times a day.

How: •••

1. **Eat like the French.** Dining in France is a celebrated activity. Adopt a European mentality and set the scene for an enjoyable meal: Pull out

the place mats or cloth napkins, put flowers or candles on the table, arrange your food on your plate, and sit down.

2. **Eliminate distractions.** Put away reading material and turn off the TV. When your body is at the table eating, let your mind be there, too. Bringing your body and mind into harmony promotes well-being.

3. **Express gratitude.** No matter what your traditions or beliefs are, creating a sacred pause to give thanks before the nourishing act of eating is a way to remember the interconnectedness of life—the planet, the farmers that grew the food, the drivers that got it to you, and the role you or someone else played in preparing it.

4. **Look before you eat.** Use a Beginner's Mind to look at the colors, textures, and details of the food on your plate as if you had never seen them before. Notice the pale green of an avocado or the way a dark red pomegranate seed bursts with juice in your mouth.

5. **Focus on flavors and aromas.** Take time to focus on the flavors in your mouth and how they interact. Pay attention to the smells. This will help you both appreciate your food and eat slower.

6. **Put your fork down between each bite.** Don't stack bites, scooping up your next mouthful when you are still chewing the last one. Putting down the fork encourages you to slow down and really taste the food (see step #5). Allow your attention to be on the food that is in your mouth instead of the food that is on your plate.

7. **Try eating in silence once in a while.** Zen master Thich Nhat Hanh recommends this in his book *Peace Is Every Step*. "Just as we turn off the TV before eating," he writes, "we can 'turn off' the talking in order to enjoy the food and the presence of one another."

48

Sip evening tea

*The ritual of a tea ceremony can be a cherished "tea meditation"
that brings you home to yourself after a busy day*

. . . .

"If only I may grow: firmer, simpler—quieter, warmer."

— Dag Hammarskjöld, diplomat, economist, author

In a small, ornate room tucked away in the Red Wall Garden Hotel in Beijing, eight of us gathered around a carved wooden table to learn the art of a Chinese tea ceremony. We were on pause during a two-day Search Inside Yourself mindfulness program, and had been told that this experience would complement our mindfulness teaching. But the ritual did more than that. We watched the tea server begin what we came to realize was an intimate dance with each of us. Her quiet mastery embodied concentration, sensitivity, grace, and timing—evident as she poured small servings into tiny cups, then refilled at the precise moment when each tea drinker was ready for more.

China is not the only culture that reveres the mindful tea ceremony. In Japan, where the tea ceremony is also tradition, it is referred to as *ichi-go ichi-e*. The phrase translates to "one time, one meeting," reminding us to embrace impermanence and honor the beauty and uniqueness in each moment. This is a mantra for tea drinking and life.

Tea meditation is one of my favorite mindfulness practices to engage in at the end of a long, busy day. It's a powerful way to cultivate awareness and serenity, which is key to winding down. We all long for connection. Sipping evening tea is a great reason to bring family and friends together. At our house, it's a form of hygge: We use a beautiful clear glass teapot that sits atop a round metal stand with a candle that warms and illuminates the liquid inside. The glowing scene is a focal point for us to encircle—and needless to say, it's cozy.

For a lesson in mindful sipping, I have to again thank my teacher, Thich Nhat Hanh. In 2013, at his Magnolia Grove Monastery in Mississippi, he taught a group of children, including my daughter, how to enjoy a tea meditation. Hundreds of adults also looked on as the elder monk moved gracefully, each gesture calm and deliberate, each movement intentional. He picked up the cup with both hands, observing the tea within it. He sipped slowly, then lowered his arms carefully. He smiled at the children to his left and right. Then he continued to drink at the same slow pace, yet keeping the silent crowd mesmerized the entire time. Our family has revered tea drinking ever since.

Try it in your home as a form of meditation through movement. That might sound counterintuitive, but just as with walking meditation, the idea is to focus on each move as you would the breath in a sitting meditation. Practice this at every step, from preparing your tea, to sitting down and noticing and appreciating the teapot, to tasting your tea and recognizing the beauty of the experience. The art of tea meditation might also become one of your favorite rituals.

How: ·

1. **Make your tea.** Find a beautiful teapot or special set of cups to use for this ritual if that adds joy to your experience. Then select your tea, heat the water, and prepare the cup. Practice meditation in motion at each step.

2. **Serve slowly.** If others are with you, look them in the eyes and then pour their tea first. This is a moment of connection. Fill the cup halfway and refill as needed, noticing when someone's cup empties.

3. **Hold your tea before drinking.** Pick up your cup with two hands to create a calm stability that is not achieved with just one hand. Notice the cup's warmth and how it makes you feel.

4. **Savor your tea.** As you begin to sip, notice the color of the liquid, the aroma, and the sensation of the drink in your mouth. You might find that paying attention to the tea makes you enjoy it more.

5. **Turn your focus inward.** Check in with yourself after a few sips. Is there any desire to hurry? Are you consumed with ideas of other things you need to do this evening? Or perhaps you feel content and peaceful. Allow your thoughts without judging them, then return your focus to the tea to resume your meditation.

6. **Take in the good.** For 15 seconds, imagine the journey your tea has taken, from leaf on a tree to the cup of delight in your hands. Give thanks for the many things that made this rejuvenating experience possible.

49

Create a bedtime routine

*Use rituals for nourishing self-care and to cue your mind
and body to wind down for sleep*

. . . .

**"Those children's bedtime rituals of supper, bath, stories, and sleep
have been a staple of my life and some of the best, most special times
I can remember."**

—Louise Brown, author

Jen gets into bed, still reading an article on her phone. An email alert
pops onto the screen, she opens it, and getting caught in the content, she
dashes off a reply to the sender. Stimulated, she starts thinking about the
meeting she needs to run the next day, and cannot get to sleep.

If any of this sounds familiar, you are not alone. According to a study
published in 2016 by the U.S. Centers for Disease Control and Prevention, about one in three Americans is sleep deprived. The study revealed
that 34.8 percent of American adults are getting less than seven hours of
sleep, the amount needed for good health and vitality.

What gets in the way of restful sleep? In our busy, technology-infused
world, it's hard to turn off a busy mind and an active body. And many
of us don't even try, as we feel compelled to cram our evenings with more
stimulating activities. Maybe it's an after-hours workout at the gym or

watching an action movie or absorbing the nightly news close to bedtime. Or maybe you indulge in a bowl of late-night ice cream or a couple of drinks to reward your hard day's work. Or perhaps you start thinking about a nagging problem, which can lead to worrying, which is a significant cause of sleeplessness.

Let's pick up with Jen. As the national managing director of well-being for the global advisory firm Deloitte, Jen is a busy professional who travels often. Given her job title, she had long ago mastered healthy eating and exercise. But her biggest challenge was getting a good night's sleep. After learning more about being present, sitting still, and meditating, she realized that the missing piece was a relaxing bedtime routine.

In the mindfulness tradition, Jen paid attention to how she was spending her evenings. You might try doing the same for a week, recording your post-dinner activities. Jen quickly recognized that she is device-addicted, and that realization enabled her to kick the habit: She now banishes her phone from her bedroom. And instead of comforting herself with food or alcohol to relax, Jen brews a cup of herbal tea, writes in her journal, dims the lights, and meditates. The biggest benefit is that the routine is independent of location—she can do it at home or in a hotel room. She says this ritual has changed her life. She now sleeps well wherever she is.

As you notice your thoughts, emotions, impulses, and habits around bedtime, you can set up your environment and develop a routine that steers you away from adverse behaviors and toward calm. Whether you hear it from a Buddhist monk or a neuroscientist, the advice is consistent: What you do at the end of the day influences your thoughts and mood—so if you want to feel peaceful, fill your final hours with activities that nourish you. If that means reading a book or listening to music or a podcast, for example, consider the content and be sure that it's soothing or uplifting, not distressing. Do things that integrate your mind and body, and that feel like a treat rather than a task.

You can spend five or 50 minutes getting ready for bed, but the key is to follow your routine consistently. As your mind and body start to associate the activities with sleep and relaxation, the routine will become a signal to let go of the day. Make sure to design a routine that suits your lifestyle so you can sustain it over time. At my house, we have shared and individual rituals. You can do both, but don't miss out on the alone time to really reconnect with yourself. After my husband, daughter, and I drink tea or go for a "pajama walk," stepping outside to take in the night air and move mindfully after dinner and homework, I try to take an aroma-therapy bath with soothing lavender scents. Plenty of men enjoy this self-care practice, too! My husband also reads a book, and my daughter reads or writes in her journal.

What might comfort and delight you at the end of the day? Light stretching, drawing or coloring, meditation? Whether you have a yoga mat, colored pencils, or a journal readily available, set yourself up so that the routine comes easily. You can set a nightly alarm reminding you that it's time to transition, and then start to slowly and lovingly lull yourself toward sleep.

How: ·

1. **Wind down an hour before bedtime.** Give your mind and body time to let go of the day. Decide on a lights-out time and subtract one hour. That's when you should start shifting gears. Set a phone alert or enlist a roommate or family member to help you stay on schedule.

2. **Go on an evening walk.** Try a walking meditation under the stars, prac-ticing open awareness. Take in the scents, sights, and sounds, and feel the air on your skin as you stroll. Gentle yoga or qigong are other options for moving and stretching before bed.

3. **Say goodnight to your devices.** Put them in their own recharging beds—far away from yours.

4. **Take stock of the day.** Recall your intentions for the day and reflect on how it went. Appreciate contributions you made, people you connected with, and any especially good moments that occurred

5. **Write in your journal.** If writing works for you, let go of the day through journaling. Record insights, reflections, and/or three things for which you are grateful. You are directing attention to the good, away from problems and worry.

6. **Soak in an aromatherapy bath.** Dim the lights, draw warm water, and add generous amounts of scented bath salts and essential oils. Relaxing your body can help your mind do the same. Activate all of your senses to fully absorb the experience.

7. **Get cuddly.** Give a loved one or roommate a long hug or snuggle with a friend, child, or pet. Touch releases soothing hormones that can promote relaxation.

50

Ease into sleep

Use your mind to relax your body for restful sleep

. . . .

"Sleep is the best meditation."

—Tenzin Gyatso, the 14th Dalai Lama

Sleep is a time of renewal, repair, and healing. You need it to flourish the next day. Neurochemical cleansing, memory consolidation, and cognitive maintenance all happen while you snooze. Think of it this way: The value of your time asleep is as important as your time awake. Getting the right amount of sleep enhances the quality of every minute you spend with your eyes open. That's why sleep is "our most underrated health habit," according to Dr. Michael Roizen, the chief wellness officer at the Cleveland Clinic. Focus, reaction speed, decision-making, spatial orientation, and more of our mental capacities suffer when we're under-slept. Sleep deprivation is also implicated in a variety of physical maladies, including high blood pressure.

General wisdom says that staying awake longer than 18 consecutive hours, or cutting back sleep to five or six hours for several nights in a row, is the threshold for these potential negative effects. Aim for seven to eight hours nightly, or experiment with the amount of rest that keeps you feeling refreshed. Then see if any of the following methods can help you stay consistent in getting what you need.

Step one might surprise you: Let go of the notion of trying to fall asleep at all. Most of us are familiar with the great irony of our relationship with sleep—that worry about getting enough of it can often be part of what keeps us awake. We can try releasing that fear with what Buddhists call "nonstriving," surrendering to the moment without wish or plan for what happens next. I think of it as acceptance, and as shifting from "doing" mode to "being" mode. Or, another reframe is that you *allow* yourself to let go of staying awake instead of *trying* to fall asleep.

You can help your body make this transition in three ways, and by now you should be well practiced in all of them. First, focus on your breath, which redirects your attention from obsessing about "me" to your body. Next, relax physically with a body scan. And, finally, try generating positive, loving, compassionate thoughts toward others.

How:

1. **Soften, soothe, and allow.** Soften your body and your breath, releasing tension. Use simple gestures to soothe yourself: You can put one hand on your heart and the other on your abdomen, or do whatever variation of this feels comforting while you follow steps 2 through 4. Allow yourself to be in bed without thoughts of being anywhere else.

2. **Rest with your breath.** Focus on the flow of air in and out of your body. Try silently saying the word "relax" or "calm" with each exhale. Feel your body gently sink into the mattress as it settles.

3. **Relax with a body scan.** The beauty of this practice is that it focuses your attention and allows you to appreciate your miraculous, wonderful body. Start at the top of your head and move downward to the bottoms of your feet, bringing your awareness to each body part and breathing into it for deeper relaxation.

4. **Extend love with prayer or a compassion practice.** Direct your attention outward by extending blessings and good wishes toward loved ones,

friends, neighbors, and in ever-widening circles, to all beings. This loving-kindness practice helps incline your mind toward benevolence and compassion. When your mind is directed away from you and focused outwardly toward others, it activates the parts of the brain associated with affiliation, belonging, and love. This positive state is a wonderful place to be before surrendering to sleep.

Sweet dreams.

Afterword

We practice mindfulness not to become masterful meditators, but to have a better life. By now you may have started experimenting with some of the strategies in this book, maybe starting your mornings with mindful breathing, doing one thing at a time at work, stepping outside for a mindful walk in nature, or seeing your loved ones with fresh eyes.

Perhaps you are noticing that you are able to maintain focus at work for a little longer before checking your phone, you recognize emotions in your body just as they begin to arise, or you approach difficult conversations with more empathy and compassion? Maybe others are noticing subtle changes in you . . . you seem a little calmer, more easygoing, more appreciative, kinder.

Whether or not you've started practicing, you might find that mindfulness is easy to learn but harder to sustain. What is the secret? Staying connected to your "why": Now that you understand the myriad benefits of mindfulness, pause right now and think about your personal reasons for picking up this book. You can start with the question, *What is it I really want?* Is it to reduce stress, to have stronger relationships, to feel your full range of emotions and live more truthfully, to be more effective at work, or to have better performance in a leisure pursuit? For many, it is to have a calm, peaceful place to go to in our hectic modern world. For me, it is to be more present, compassionate, and loving. It often comes down to love.

Write your reasons on a sticky note so you can keep them top of mind. Look to it for inspiration whenever you need it. Becoming more mindful is an ongoing process. Start small and build up from there. Begin by remembering to stop and breathe, to come home to the present moment with an open mind and heart, at any time during the day. It *is* that simple. As your self-awareness increases, you will become more familiar with recognizing what you are experiencing and knowing which mindfulness practice will deepen your experience or create more space. Remember the analogy of learning to ski? With mindfulness you first learn the basics, then you practice, and find yourself applying it to everyday situations, then on to handling stronger emotions, bigger challenges, and you soon find yourself calmer, experiencing more joy and less stress, in more and more moments of your day.

Wherever you are in your own journey toward integrating mindfulness into your life, do so with a mindset of curiosity, kindness, and wonder. Remember that you are embracing the freeing, empowering effect of being able to deliberately direct your attention on demand—to cultivate a positive outlook infused with compassion for yourself and others. An adage that I often turn to is, *We do for ourselves, so that we can do for others.* It can be inspiring to know that when you do something positive like becoming more mindful—more present, aware, insightful, and compassionate—it benefits you and everyone in your life. So what is it that you really want? Whatever it is, mindfulness can help you get there.

Recommended Resources

Mindfulness meditation is a self-driven activity, much like exercise. But you don't have to go it alone. You can check out digital apps, online resources, teachers, groups, and practice centers to support you, deepen your learning, and offer encouragement. Remember, though, that mindfulness can be applied to the everyday activities that you already do, so with this book as a guide you can always find time to practice.

Listen to Guided Meditation Audio

Having the voice of an experienced teacher in your ear can be very helpful in providing support for the foundational training practices of mindful breathing, loving-kindness meditation, and the body scan, to name a few. You might find it extra helpful as you get started, and for many of us it is an integral part of sustaining a practice anytime, anywhere. The mobile app I most recommend is Insight Timer—you have access to guided meditations from a variety of teachers and a set of beautiful digital bells you can use to time your meditation session for however long you like, you can join groups and connect with friends, and it is free! You might also try the 10% Happier app for short teaching videos along with guided audio, Calm and Headspace, popular apps for getting started, both of which are paid subscription services after you complete the basics.

Find a Good Teacher

Like learning to play a musical instrument or master a sport, you can benefit from having a skilled, experienced teacher for targeted feedback, working with challenges, and answering specific questions. It is important to choose credentialed teachers with a long-term practice of their own, and teachers with whom you have good chemistry to foster a relationship of mutual trust, respect, and caring. The Search Inside Yourself Leadership Institute *(siyli.org)* posts credentialed teachers—graduates of its rigorous year-long program, which was the springboard for much of my mindfulness work. The UCLA Mindful Awareness Research Center *(marc.ucla .edu)* also posts graduates of its year-long training program. Tara Brach and Jack Kornfield are currently leading a comprehensive two-year program called the Mindfulness Meditation Teacher Certification Program *(soundstrue.com)*—of which I am also a part.

Practice With Others

Create and practice in a community, a powerful way to sustain and integrate mindfulness into your life. Many of our corporate clients (banks, high-tech, consulting) have set up weekly or monthly drop-in meditation sessions right in the office. Use an email distribution list and post a schedule, and you can meet up in a reserved conference room or join online. Simply select a guided audio meditation and hit play, or have someone guide it live. It will be easy to experience the peaceful energy in the room (or online) as you sit together, which can inspire and encourage you to keep going—and hanging out with others will enrich your life (remember "Gather your posse")? If you work independently or remotely, you can join a virtual group, such as the Telesangha *(telesangha.com)* or make a regular virtual date with a friend.

Enjoy a Mindfulness Retreat

Reward yourself with the experience of a dedicated time to learn, grow, heal, and even transform your life by swapping your usual vacation plan with a mindfulness retreat. Here you'll find a mix of teaching sessions, guided meditations, walking meditation, and free time for your own practice in a supportive community away from the daily hustle. Whether it is an afternoon in the middle of the city (I recently joined an urban retreat with the Consciousness Explorers Club in Toronto) or a weekend or 10-day getaway, consider giving yourself time away that might provide more sustainable joy than standing in line at a tourist destination. My favorites are the mindfulness practice centers in the tradition of Thich Nhat Hanh: Magnolia Grove in Mississippi, Deer Park in California, Blue Cliff in New York, and the main monastery at Plum Village near Bordeaux, France, which are especially great for families and groups of friends. For individual practice, you can check out those held by the Insight Meditation centers in Washington, D.C., Massachusetts, and California, and the Inward Bound Mindfulness Education (IBMe) retreats for teens are an immersive adventure in mindfulness without parents around.

Get Specific Mindfulness Training

You might appreciate mindfulness programs tailored for your group, interest, or need. There are mindfulness programs designed for specific audiences and purposes, such as CARE for Teachers (Cultivating Awareness and Resilience in Education); Mindful Practice for Physicians by the University of Rochester Medical Center; Search Inside Yourself Leadership Institute for the mindfulness training program developed at Google and teacher certification; PurposeBlue Mindful Leadership for corporate mindfulness training, one-on-one coaching, and conference keynotes; Mindful Self-Compassion with Christopher Germer and Kristin Neff; Mindfulness-Based Childbirth and Parenting (MBCP) classes; and Judson Brewer's Craving to Quit—a mindfulness-based program with accompanying apps: one for smoking cessation and one called Eat Right Now for creating healthier eating habits.

Acknowledgments

This book is a testament to the generosity of the people in my life: family, friends, colleagues, students, and clients. We are all interconnected, and this book is a work of love that comes from their collective wisdom and support.

I am honored to work with the team at National Geographic. Hilary Black, this book came into being because of your vision and clear commitment to bringing mindfulness to busy professionals. A big thank you to Anne Smyth for your skillful editing, warm encouragement, and smart suggestions. You brought this book to another level. I am grateful to the work of editors Kate Armstrong and Heather McElwain. Thank you to Daneen Goodwin and Jessie Chirico in marketing and social media; to Ann Day and Kelly Forsythe in PR and communications; and to Bill O'Donnell in sales.

I am eternally grateful to Lena Tabori, who championed and mentored me from day one to the final evening of writing in her guesthouse. You are an inspiration to me. This book would not be here without the expertise, intellectual guidance, and mentoring from Marya Dalrymple. Marya helped me shape the book, develop first drafts, and hone my voice while fiercely challenging me and compassionately encouraging me throughout the project. My gratitude runs deep.

I am deeply grateful to the loving and peaceful Chau Yoder, a senior teacher with Thich Nhat Hanh, who introduced me to mindfulness 22 years ago and has taught and encouraged me ever since; and to our teacher, Thich Nhat Hanh (Thay), especially for taking my daughter's hand in his and teaching our family to "kiss the earth" with each step, to see the cloud in our tea, to smile, come home to the breath, and to be present for each other. I am grateful for the years of learning and inspiration from Tara Brach, and now as a student of Tara and Jack Kornfield as a team, for how they model the way.

Thank you to the teachers whose lessons in the science of mindfulness and compassion I have been fortunate to experience: Richie Davidson, Dan Siegel, Rick Hanson, Shauna Shapiro, Hooria Jazaieri, Tania Singer, Christopher Germer, and Kristin Neff. Thank you Otto Scharmer at MIT's Presencing Institute for teaching me about the field, presence, and sensing, and my mindful coaching teachers Doug Silsbee and Bebe Hansen from the Presence-based Leadership Institute.

Thay teaches us to "go like a river" in a *sangha*. I am deeply grateful for my practice with his sanghas of Plum Village and Magnolia Grove, which show us how to live in a loving, mindful community, and for the Insight Meditation Community of Washington here at home. I am grateful to my tribe at the Search Inside Yourself Leadership Institute (SIYLI), where I learned from Chade-Meng Tan, Marc Lesser, and Meg Levie ways to translate mindfulness into evidence-based, accessible language for the modern world. To my co-teachers Lori Schwanbeck, Hemant Bhanoo, Simon Moyes, Robert Chender, Mark Coleman, Peter Weng, Brandon Rennels, Dana Pulley, and Paul Mentag: I have learned much witnessing you in action. I am indebted to the community of students who shared their questions, stories, and insights during the writing of this book. And for my newest sangha, I am thankful for the learning in our cohort of mindfulness teachers led by Tara and Jack as we repeatedly come together among the redwoods at the 1440 Multiversity.

Thank you to Rob Sheehan for being an early adopter of mindfulness in higher education and inviting me to bring Mindful Leadership to the University of Maryland's Robert H. Smith School of Business every year. And thank you to Nance Lucas and Beth Cabrera for my role as a Senior Fellow at the Center for the Advancement of Well-Being at George Mason University.

I am grateful to teacher Julie Quintana and the school communities at Chevy Chase Elementary, North Chevy Chase Elementary, and Somerset and Carderock Springs Elementary Schools in Maryland for partnering with me in teaching mindfulness to their faculties, students, and parents, and helping us reinforce—in more than 2,000 children—their innate capacities for positivity, joy, and kindness.

To my mentor Susan Butler, thank you for the advice and opportunities at Accenture and for the last 25 years. Thank you to Deloitte's Jen Fisher and her team for choosing PurposeBlue to bring our Mindful Leader program to the firm across North America. A big thank you to Elizabeth Ouren and Daisy Hilliard for managing our PurposeBlue mindfulness programs with excellence and warmth during this busy year, and for building our community of students, clients, readers, and friends and supporting the book along the way.

Thank you to Heide Leben, Friedrich Meyer, Annika Botved, and Julia von Richthofen for teaching me how to infuse life with art, *hygge*, beauty, and ritual. And for teaching me how to create flow while making art: thank you to Gunnar Klenke and our painting group. Thank you to Pedro Marquez Diaz for inspiration; to Scott Morgan and our spiritual storytelling group for truth; to the BS7 for encouraging me to shine; and to Katharina Aust, Michelle Fontaine, Cameron Bach, Gianna Vallefuoco, and Anne Teather for unending loving connection. Serena Chreky, thank you for the thousand acts of kindness during this project, like when you knew I was tucked away writing at the Jefferson Hotel library bar and you phoned the hotel and secretly paid for my lunch. Elizabeth Kivimae, thank you for showing me 20 years ago the power of meditation, and for walking closely with me through this book, as well as my life.

I am thankful for the sheltered spaces of seclusion where I could cultivate the flow of writing, especially Donia's Jaufentalerhof in the Alps; our family's rustic, remote Tuscan house; my niece Charlotte and her husband, Hendrick's, peaceful horse ranch in Germany; and Lena's Swedish-inspired guesthouse.

I am nourished by the love and encouragement of my extended family in the United States and Germany. Thank you especially to my sister, Karen Helms, for your gift with language and big-sister belief in me, and to sister-friend Natasha Tabori Fried for giving my family your generous love, care, and support.

I was profoundly shaped by the experience of growing up with my gentle brother, the talented artist and wise soul John Cameron. He met everyone with his heart wide open. Thank you, Johnny, for believing in me, loving me, and seeing me so clearly. You told me to stop only consuming other people's creations and use my time on Earth to produce my own. This is for you.

Thank you to my late father, John W. Cameron, who gave me early experiences of wonder, awe, and transcendence at his thundering NASA rocket launches in the desert. I am eternally grateful to my late mother, Anne, the most spiritual and altruistic person I know, for raising me with the sacred, and for showing me the daily practices of sitting in stillness, contemplative study, journaling, ongoing prayer, and commitment to service. You were right, Mom, you are always with me.

For my daughter, Ava Grace: Thank you for being with me in the serenity and smiles of the monasteries, rewriting the meditations for your classmates, being the bell master in our family sangha, and giving me sweet and loving encouragement throughout this intense process. Thank you for jumping into this with me—mapping out the book on my whiteboard in colored pens, editing with Daddy, and giving me smart feedback and good ideas. You inspire me. You are my heart.

And finally, for my husband Andreas Guessmann. Thank you for 20 adventurous years of marriage, and for being my partner in bringing our miracle Ava Grace into the world. You show us what calm, quiet steadiness looks like, and I am grateful for your caring support and kindness, and for the love that we share.

Selected Sources

INTRODUCTION

Congleton, Christina, Britta K. Hölzel, and Sara W. Lazar, "Mindfulness Can Literally Change Your Brain," *Harvard Business Review,* January 8, 2015. hbr.org/2015/01/mindfulness-can-literally-change-your-brain.

Dalai Lama, Desmond Tutu, and Douglas Carlton Abrams. *The Book of Joy.* New York: Avery, 2016.

Emmons, R. A., and M. E. McCullough. "Counting Blessings Versus Burdens: An Experimental Investigation of Gratitude and Subjective Well-Being in Daily Life." *Journal of Personality and Social Psychology* 84, no. 2 (2010).

Good, Darren J., et al. "Contemplating Mindfulness at Work: An Integrative Review." *Journal of Management* 42, no. 1 (2016): 114–142. journals.sagepub.com/doi/abs/10.1177/0149206315617003.

Hanh, Thich Nhat. *The Miracle of Mindfulness.* Boston: Beacon Press, 1999.

———. *Peace Is Every Step: The Path of Mindfulness in Everyday Life.* New York: Bantam, 1992.

Hölzel, B. K., et al. "How Does Mindfulness Meditation Work? Proposing Mechanisms of Action From a Conceptual and Neural Perspective." *Perspectives in Psychological Science* 6 (2011): 537–559.

Kabat-Zinn, Jon. *Wherever You Go, There You Are: Mindfulness Meditation in Everyday Life.* New York: Hyperion, 1994.

Katie, Byron. *Loving What Is.* New York: Harmony, 2002.

Killingsworth, Matthew A., and Daniel T. Gilbert. "A Wandering Mind Is an Unhappy Mind." *Science* 330, no. 6006 (2010): 932.

Klimecki, O. M., S. Leiberg, M. Ricard, and T. Singer. "Differential Pattern of Functional Brain Plasticity after Compassion and Empathy Training." *Social Cognitive and Affective Neuroscience* 9, no. 6 (2014). doi:10.1093/scan/nst060.

Kornfield, Jack. *No Time Like the Present.* New York: Atria, 2017.

Lutz, J., et al. "Mindfulness and Emotion Regulation—an fMRI Study." *Social Cognitive and Affective Neuroscience* 9 (2014): 776–785.

Nash, Jonathan D., and Andrew Newberg. "Toward a Unifying Taxonomy and Definition for Meditation." *Frontiers in Psychology* 4 (2013): 806.

Pagnoni, G., and M. Cekic. "Age Effects on Gray Matter Volume and Attentional Performance in Zen Meditation." *Neurobiology of Aging* 28, no. 10 (2007): 1623–1627. Published online July 25, 2007. doi:10.1016/j.neurobiolaging.2007.06.008.

Salzberg, Sharon. *Real Love.* New York: Flatiron Books, 2017.

Seligman, Martin E. P., and John Tierney. "We Aren't Built to Live in the Moment." *New York Times,* May 19, 2017. nytimes.com/2017/05/19/opinion/sunday/why-the -future-is-always-on-your-mind.html.

Tang, Yi-Yuan, Britta K. Hölzel, and Michael I. Posner. "The Neuroscience of Mindfulness Meditation." *Nature Reviews Neuroscience* 16 (2015): 213–225. Published online March 18, 2015. doi: 10.1038/nrn3916.

Warren, Jeff. "Jeff Warren & the '10% Happier' Road Trip." Interview by Dan Harris, *10% Happier,* podcast #57, January 20, 2017.

"What Is Compassion?" *Greater Good Magazine.* Greater Good Science Center at UC Berkeley. greatergood.berkeley.edu/compassion/definition.

HOME: Start the Day

Baraz, James, and Shoshana Alexander. *Awakening Joy: 10 Steps to Happiness.* Berkeley, CA: Parallax Press, 2010.

Bash, Barbara. "The Simple Joy of Writing by Hand." *Mindful,* June 3, 2016. mindful .org/the-simple-joy-of-writing-by-hand/.

Cameron, Julia. *The Artist's Way: A Spiritual Path to Higher Creativity.* New York: Penguin, 1992.

Duhigg, Charles. *The Power of Habit: Why We Do What We Do in Life and Business.* New York: Random House, 2012.

Gino, Francesca, and Adam Grant. "The Big Benefits of a Little Thanks." HBR IdeaCast. *Harvard Business Review.* hbr.org/2013/11/the-big-benefits-of-a-little-thanks.

Grant, Adam, and Francesca Gino. "A Little Thanks Goes a Long Way: Explaining Why Gratitude Expressions Motivate Prosocial Behavior." *Journal of Personality and Social Psychology* 98, no. 6 (2010): 946–955.

Hanh, Thich Nhat. *The Miracle of Mindfulness.* Boston: Beacon Press, 1975.

Hanson, Rick. *Hardwiring Happiness: The New Brain Science of Contentment, Calm, and Confidence.* New York: Harmony, 2013.

Helliwell, John F., Richard Layard, and Jeffrey Sachs, eds. *World Happiness Report 2015.* New York: Sustainable Development Solutions Network, 2015.

Hempton, Gordon. "Silence and the Presence of Everything." Interview by Krista Tippett. *On Being,* December 29, 2016. onbeing.org/programs/gordon-hempton-silence -and-the-presence-of-everything/.

Jinpa, Thupten. *A Fearless Heart: How the Courage to Be Compassionate Can Transform Our Lives.* New York: Hudson Street Press, 2015.

Kabat-Zinn, Jon. *Coming to Our Senses: Healing Ourselves and the World Through Mindfulness.* New York: Hyperion, 2005.

Mills, Billy, Christina Torres, Ashley Hicks, et al. "Running as Spiritual Practice." Interview by Krista Tippett. *On Being,* August 18, 2016. onbeing.org/programs/billy-mills -christina-torres-ashley-hicks-et-al-running-as-spiritual-practice/.

Seppälä, Emma. *The Happiness Track: How to Apply the Science of Happiness to Accelerate Your Success.* New York: Harper One, 2016.

Siegel, Dan. "Wheel of Awareness." drdansiegel.com/resources/wheel_of_awareness/.

Tsafou, Kalliopi-Eleni, D. De Ridder, R. van Ee, and J. Lacroix. "Mindfulness and Satisfaction in Physical Activity." *Journal of Health Psychology* 21, no. 9 (2015): 1817–1827.

WORK: Seize the Day

Brach, Tara. *Radical Acceptance: Embracing Your Life With the Heart of a Buddha.* New York: Random House, 2003.

———. "Your Future Self: Turning Towards Your Awakened HeartMind." Podcast. tarabrach.com/your-future-self/.

Brewer, J. A., P. D. Worhunsky, J. R. Gray, Y. Y. Tang, J. Weber, and H. Kober. "Meditation Experience Is Associated With Differences in Default Mode Network Activity and Connectivity." *Proceedings of the National Academy of Sciences* 108, no. 50 (2011): 20254–20259.

Brewer, Judson. *The Craving Mind: From Cigarettes to Smartphones to Love—Why We Get Hooked and How We Can Break Bad Habits.* New Haven, CT: Yale University Press, 2017.

Cameron, Laurie J. "A Mindful Approach to Navigating Strategic Change." In *The Neuroscience of Learning and Development,* edited by Marilee J. Bresciani Ludvik, 289–308. Sterling, VA: Stylus Publishing, 2016.

Chatterjee, Debashis. *Leading Consciously: A Pilgrimage Toward Self-Mastery.* Woburn, MA: Butterworth-Heineman, 1998.

Chui, M., et al. "The Social Economy: Unlocking Value and Productivity Through Social Technologies." McKinsey Global Institute. McKinsey & Company, July 2012.

Csikszentmihalyi, Mihaly. *Flow: The Psychology of Optimal Experience.* New York: Harper Perennial, 1990.

Davidson, Richard, and Sharon Begley. *The Emotional Life of Your Brain: How Its Unique Patterns Affect the Way You Think, Feel, and Live—and How You Can Change Them.* New York: Hudson Street Press, 2012.

Dutton, J. E., K. M. Workman, and A. E. Hardin. "Compassion at Work." Cornell University, School of Hotel Administration. The Scholarly Commons, 2014. scholarship .sha.cornell.edu/cgi/viewcontent.cgi?article=1733&context=articles.

Farb, Norman A. S., Zindel V. Segal, Helen Mayberg, Jim Bean, Deborah McKeon, Zainab Fatima, and Adam K. Anderson. "Attending to the Present: Mindfulness Meditation

Reveals Distinct Neural Modes of Self-Reference." *Social Cognitive and Affective Neuroscience* 2 no. 4 (2007): 313–322. doi:10.1093/scan/nsm030.

Frederickson, B. L., and C. Branigan. "Positive Emotions Broaden the Scope of Attention and Thought-Action Repertoires." *Cognition and Emotion* 19 (2005): 313–332.

Garrett, Montgomery E. "What's the Secret of the Best Places to Work? Compassion and Connection." *Success,* October 27, 2015. success.com/article/whats-the-secret-of-the-best-places-to-work-compassion-and-connection.

Goleman, Daniel and Richard J. Davidson. *Altered Traits: Science Reveals How Meditation Changes Your Mind, Brain, and Body.* New York: Avery, 2017.

Good, Darren J., et al. "Contemplating Mindfulness at Work: An Integrative Review." *Journal of Management* 42 (2015): 1–29.

Gross, James J. "The Emerging Field of Emotion Regulation: An Integrative Review." *Review of General Psychology* 2, no. 3 (1998): 271–299.

Harris, Dan. *10 Percent Happier: How I Tamed the Voice in My Head, Reduced Stress Without Losing My Edge, and Found Self-Help That Actually Works—A True Story.* New York: HarperCollins, 2014.

Hülsheger, U. R., H. J. Alberts, A. Reinholdt, and J. W. Lang. "Benefits of Mindfulness at Work: The Role of Mindfulness in Emotion Regulation, Emotional Exhaustion, and Job Satisfaction." *Journal of Applied Psychology.* researchgate.net/publication/234018520_Benefits_of_Mindfulness_at_Work_The_Role_of_Mindfulness_in_Emotion_Regulation_Emotional_Exhaustion_and_Job_Satisfaction.

Hutcherson, Cendri A., Emma M. Seppälä, and James J. Gross. "Loving-Kindness Meditation Increases Social Connectedness." *Emotion* 8, no. 5 (2008): 720.

Jaworski, Joseph. *The Inner Path of Leadership.* San Francisco: Berrett-Koehler Publishers, 1996.

Jazaieri, Hooria, Ihno A. Lee, Kelly McGonigal, Thupten Jinpa, James R. Doty, James J. Gross, and Philippe R. Goldin. "A Wandering Mind Is a Less Caring Mind: Daily Experience Sampling During Compassion Meditation Training." *The Journal of Positive Psychology* 11 (2016).

Killingsworth, Matthew A., and Danial T. Gilbert. "A Wandering Mind Is an Unhappy Mind." *Science* 12, no. 330 (2010): 932.

Kim, Larry. "Multitasking Is Killing Your Brain." *Inc.* Last modified July 15, 2015. inc.com/larry-kim/why-multi-tasking-is-killing-your-brain.html.

Lazar, Sarah, et al. "Meditation Experience Is Associated With Increased Cortical Thickness." *NeuroReport* 16, no. 17 (2005): 1893–1897.

Levitin, Daniel J. "Why the Modern World Is Bad for Your Brain." *Guardian,* January 18, 2015. theguardian.com/science/2015/jan/18/modern-world-bad-for-brain-daniel-j-levitin-organized-mind-information-overload.

McGonigal, Kelly. *The Neuroscience of Change: A Compassion-Based Program for Personal Transformation.* Louisville, CO: Sounds True, 2012.

————. *The Upside of Stress: Why Stress Is Good for You, and How to Get Good at It.* New York: Penguin, 2015.

Miller Lab. "Time.com—You Asked: Are My Devices Messing With My Brain?" *In the News,* May 18, 2015. ekmillerlab.mit.edu/2015/05/18/time-com-you-asked -are-my-devices-messing-with-my-brain/.

Schaefer, Stacey M., et al. "Purpose in Life Predicts Better Emotional Recovery From Negative Stimuli." *PLoS One* 8, no. 11 (2013). journals.plos.org/plosone/article?id=10 .1371/journal.pone.0080329.

Scharmer, C. Otto. *Theory U: Leading From the Future As It Emerges.* San Francisco: Berrett-Koehler Publishers, 2009, 2016.

Schulte, Brigid. *Overwhelmed: Work, Love, and Play When No One Has the Time.* New York: Picador, 2014.

Seligman, Martin. *Flourish: A Visionary New Understanding of Happiness and Well-Being.* New York: Atria, 2011.

Seligman, Martin E. P. *Authentic Happiness: Using the New Positive Psychology to Realize Your Potential for Lasting Fulfillment.* New York: Simon & Schuster, 2002.

Seligman, Martin E. P., and John Tierney. "We Aren't Built to Live in the Moment." *New York Times,* last modified May 19, 2017. nytimes.com/2017/05/19/opinion/sunday/ why-the-future-is-always-on-your-mind.html.

Seppälä, Emma. "Social Connection and Compassion: Important Predictors of Health and Well-Being." *Social Research* 80, no. 2 (2013): 411–430.

Sheldon, K., and Sonja Lyubomirsky. "How to Increase and Sustain Positive Emotion: The Effects of Expressing Gratitude and Visualizing Best Possible Selves." *Journal of Positive Psychology* 1, no. 2 (2006): 73–82.

Singer, Tania. "The Neuroscience of Compassion." Presentation at the World Economic Forum, March 9, 2015. Video. youtube.com/watch?v=n-hKS4rucTY.

Tan, Chade-Meng. *Search Inside Yourself: The Unexpected Path to Achieving Success, Happiness (and World Peace).* New York: HarperCollins, 2012.

Teper, Rimma, Zindel V. Segal, and Michael Inzlicht. "Inside the Mindful Mind: How Mindfulness Enhances Emotion Regulation Through Improvements in Executive Control." *Current Directions in Psychological Science* 22, no. 6 (2013): 449–454.

University of Cambridge. "Gut Feelings Help Make More Successful Financial Traders." *Science Daily,* July 30, 2017. sciencedaily.com/releases/2016/09/160918214445 .htm.

Ward, Adrian F., Kristen Duke, Ayelet Gneezy, and Maarten W. Bos. "Brain Drain: The Mere Presence of One's Own Smartphone Reduces Available Cognitive Capacity." *Journal of the Association for Consumer Research* 2, no. 2 (2017): 140–154.

Wilson, Timothy D., and Daniel T. Gilbert. "Affective Forecasting: Knowing What We Want." *Current Direction in Psychological Science* 14 (2005): 131–134.

Worline, Monica, and J. E. Dutton. *Awakening Compassion at Work: The Quiet Power That Elevates People and Organizations.* Oakland, CA: Berrett-Koehler Publishers, 2017.

PLAY: Enrich the Day

Berman, Marc G., John Jonides, and Stephen Kaplan. "The Cognitive Benefits of Interacting With Nature." *Psychological Science* 19, no. 12 (2008): 1207–1212.

Bratman, G. N., G. Daily, B. Levy, and J. J. Gross. "The Benefits of Nature Experience: Improved Affect and Cognition." *Landscape and Urban Planning* 138 (2015): 41–50.

Brown, Stuart, and Christopher Vaughan. *Play: How It Shapes the Brain, Opens the Imagination, and Invigorates the Soul.* New York: Avery, 2010.

Cameron, Julia. *The Artist's Way: A Spiritual Path to Higher Creativity.* New York: Penguin, 1992.

Chanda, Mona Lisa, and Daniel J. Levitin. "The Neurochemistry of Music." *Trends in Cognitive Sciences* 17, no. 4 (2013): 178–193.

Chen, Yu. "Promoting Positive Affect Through Smartphone Photography." *Psychology of Well-Being* 6, no. 8 (2016).

Csikszentmihalyi, Mihaly. *Flow: The Psychology of Optimal Experience.* New York: Harper Perennial, 1990.

Diehl, Kristen, Gal Zauberman, and Alixandra Barasch. "How Taking Photos Increases Enjoyment and Experiences." *Journal of Personality and Social Psychology* 111, no. 2 (2016): 119–140.

Gilbert, Elizabeth. "Choosing Curiosity Over Fear." Interview by Krista Tippett. *On Being,* July 7, 2016. Podcast audio, 51:00. onbeing.org/programs/elizabeth-gilbert-choosing-curiosity-over-fear/.

Hanh, Thich Nhat. *How to Walk.* Berkeley, CA: Parallax Press, 2015.

———. *Planting Seeds: Practicing Mindfulness With Children.* Berkeley, CA: Parallax Press, 2011.

Juyoung Lee, Yuko Tsunetsugu, Norimasa Takayama, and Yoshifumi Miyazaki. "Influence of Forest Therapy on Cardiovascular Relaxation in Young Adults." *Evidence-Based Complementary and Alternative Medicine* (February 2014).

Katie, Byron, and Stephen Mitchell. *A Mind at Home With Itself: How Asking Four Questions Can Free Your Mind, Open Your Heart, and Turn Your World Around.* New York: Harper One, 2017.

Kaya, Sabri. "The Relationship Between Leisure Satisfaction and Happiness Among College Students." *Universal Journal of Educational Research* 4, no. 3 (2016): 622–631.

Lyubomirsky, S., and H. Lepper. "A Measure of Subjective Happiness: Preliminary Reliability and Construct Validation." *Social Indicators Research* 46, no. 2 (1999): 137–155.

Milkie, Melissa A., Kei Nomaguchi, and Kathleen E. Denny. "Does the Amount of Time Mothers Spend With Children or Adolescents Matter?" *Journal of Marriage and Family* 77, no. 2 (2015): 355–372.

Schulte, Brigid. "Making Time for Kids? Study Says Quality Trumps Quantity." *Washington Post,* last modified March 25, 2015. www.washingtonpost.com/local/making-time

-for-kids-study-says-quality-trumps-quantity/2015/03/28/10813192-d378-11e4-8fce
-3941fc548f1c_story.html?utm_term=.37471c212e38.

Suttie, Jill. "How Nature Can Make You Kinder, Happier, and More Creative." *Greater Good Magazine,* March 2, 2016. Greater Good Science Center at UC Berkeley. greatergood.berkeley.edu/article/item/how_nature_makes_you_kinder_happier_more_creative.

Trent University. "Your Happiness Could Depend on the Time You Spend Outdoors." *Daily News,* July 12, 2016. http://www.trentu.ca/newsevents/newsDetail.php?news Id=15885.

Weintraub, Karen. "Museum Visits Can Promote Mindfulness." *Boston Globe,* June 26, 2015. bostonglobe.com/lifestyle/2015/06/26/visits-museums-can-promote-mindfulness/0GzK269SyqY1gFVYJQU2fL/story.html.

Williams, Florence. "This Is Your Brain on Nature." *National Geographic.* nationalgeographic.com/magazine/2016/01/call-to-wild/.

LOVE: Embrace the Day

Baraz, James, and Michele Lilyanna. *Awakening Joy for Kids.* Berkeley, CA: Parallax Press, 2016.

Brach, Tara. *True Refuge: Finding Peace and Freedom in Your Own Awakened Heart.* New York: Bantam, 2013.

Chödrön, Pema. *When Things Fall Apart: Heart Advice for Difficult Times.* Boulder, CO: Shambhala Publications, 2000.

Coan, J. A., H. Schaefer, and R. J. Davidson. "Lending a Hand: Social Regulation of the Neural Response to Threat." *Psychological Science* 17, no. 12 (2006): 1032–1039.

Cornell, Ann Weiser. *The Power of Focusing: A Practical Guide to Emotional Self-Healing.* Oakland, CA: New Harbinger, 1996.

Frederickson, Barbara. "Open Hearts Build Lives: Positive Emotions, Induced Through Loving-Kindness Meditation." *Journal of Personality and Social Psychology* 95, no. 5 (2008): 1045–1062.

Germer, Christopher. *The Mindful Path to Self-Compassion: Freeing Yourself From Destructive Thoughts and Emotions.* New York: Guilford Press, 2009.

Grewen, K. M., B. J. Anderson, S. S. Girdler, and K. C. Light. "Warm Partner Contact Is Related to Lower Cardiovascular Reactivity." *Behavioral Medicine* 23, no. 3 (2003): 123–130.

Hanh, Thich Nhat. *How to Love.* Berkeley, CA: Parallax Press, 2014.

———. *Joyfully Together: The Art of Building a Harmonious Community.* Berkeley, CA: Parallax Press, 2009.

———. *True Love: A Practice for Awakening the Heart.* Boston: Shambhala Publications, 2011.

Khong, Chan. *Beginning Anew: Four Steps to Restoring Communication.* Berkeley, CA: Parallax Press, 2014.

Kok, B. E., L. Catalino, and B. Fredrickson. "How Positive Emotions Build Physical Health: Perceived Positive Social Connections Account for the Upward Spiral Between Positive Emotions and Vagal Tone." *Psychological Science* 24, no. 7 (2013): 1123–1132.

Kornfield, Jack. *The Wise Heart: A Guide to the Universal Teachings of Buddhist Psychology.* New York: Random House, 2008.

Neff, Kristin. *Self-Compassion: Stop Beating Yourself Up and Leave Insecurity Behind.* New York: HarperCollins, 2011.

Ostaseski, Frank. *The Five Invitations: Discovering What Death Can Teach Us About Living Fully.* New York: Flatiron Books, 2017.

Singer, Tania, and Olga Klimecki. "Empathy and Compassion." *Current Biology* 24, no. 18 (2014): R875–R878.

Trudeau, Michelle. "Human Connections Start With a Friendly Touch." *Morning Edition,* September 20, 2010. Podcast audio, 3:35. npr.org/templates/story/story.php?storyId=128795325.

Zaki, Jamil, and Kevin N. Ochsner. "The Neuroscience of Empathy: Progress, Pitfalls and Promise." *Nature Neuroscience* 15, no. 5 (2012): 675–680.

HOME: End the Day

Altman, Anna. "The Year of Hygge, the Danish Obsession With Getting Cozy." *New Yorker,* December 18, 2016. newyorker.com/culture/culture-desk/the-year-of-hygge-the-danish-obsession-with-getting-cozy.

Brits, Louisa Thomsen. *The Book of Hygge: The Danish Art of Contentment, Comfort, and Connection.* New York: Plume, 2016.

Centers for Disease Control and Prevention. "1 in 3 Adults Don't Get Enough Sleep." U.S. Department of Health and Human Services, press release, February 18, 2016. cdc.gov/media/releases/2016/p0215-enough-sleep.html.

Emmons, R. A., and R. Stern. "Gratitude as a Psychotherapeutic Intervention." *Journal of Clinical Psychology* 69, no. 8 (2013): 846–855.

Fisher, Jen. "Interview with Jen Fisher." February 1, 2017.

Fredrickson, Barbara. "What Good Are Positive Emotions?" *Review of General Psychology* 2, no. 3 (1998): 300–319.

Hanh, Thich Nhat. *How to Eat.* Berkeley, CA: Parallax Press, 2014.

———. *Peace Is Every Step: The Path of Mindfulness in Everyday Life.* New York: Bantam, 1992.

Huffington, Arianna. *The Sleep Revolution: Transforming Your Life, One Night at a Time.* New York: Harmony Books, 2016.

Keltner, Dacher. "Hands On Research: The Science of Touch." *Greater Good Magazine,* September 29, 2010. Greater Good Science Center at UC Berkeley. greatergood.berkeley.edu/article/item/hands_on_research.

Kondo, Marie. *The Life-Changing Magic of Tidying Up: The Japanese Art of Decluttering and Organizing.* Berkeley, CA: Ten Speed Press, 2014.

Liu, Yong, et al. "Prevalence of Healthy Sleep Duration Among Adults." *Morbidity and Mortality Weekly Report* 65, no. 6 (2016): 137–141.

Sonnentag, S., C. Binnewies, and E. J. Mojza. "Did You Have a Nice Evening?" A Day-Level Study on Recovery Experiences, Sleep, and Affect." *Journal of Applied Psychology* 93, no. 3 (2008): 674–684.

Wiking, Meik. *The Little Book of Hygge: Danish Secrets to Happy Living.* New York: Harper Collins, 2017.

Index